OLD TESTAMENT GU

General Editor

R.N. Whybray

MICAH, NAHUM, OBADIAH

Other titles in this series include

THE SECOND ISAIAH
R.N. Whybray

EXODUS
W. Johnstone

1 AND 2 SAMUEL
R.P. Gordon

PSALMS
J. Day

JUDGES
A.D.H. Mayes

GENESIS 1-11
J.W. Rogerson

DANIEL
P.R. Davies

JOB
J.H. Eaton

AMOS
A.G. Auld

EZRA AND NEHEMIAH
H.G.M. Williamson

HAGGAI, ZECHARIAH, MALACHI
R.J. Coggins

JEREMIAH
R.P. Carroll

ECCLESIASTES
R.N. Whybray

DEUTERONOMY
R.E. Clements

THE SONG OF SONGS
A. Brenner

MICAH
NAHUM
OBADIAH

R. Mason

Published by JSOT Press
for the Society for Old Testament Study

Copyright © 1991 Sheffield Academic Press

Published by JSOT Press
JSOT Press is an imprint of
Sheffield Academic Press Ltd
The University of Sheffield
343 Fulwood Road
Sheffield S10 3BP
England

Printed on acid-free paper in Great Britain
by Billing & Sons Ltd
Worcester

British Library Cataloguing in Publication Data

Mason, Rex
    Micah, Nahum, Obadiah.
    1. Christianity. Scriptures   2. Judaism. Scriptures
    I. Title   II. Series
    224.9

    ISSN 0264-6498
    ISBN 1-85075-702-X

CONTENTS

88499

ABBREVIATIONS

ATD	Das Alte Testament Deutsch, Göttingen
AV	Authorized Version (King James Version)
BJRL	*Bulletin of the John Rylands Library,* Manchester
BK	Biblischer Kommentar, Neukirchen
BZ	*Biblische Zeitschrift,* Freiburg, Paderborn
BZAW	Beihefte zur *Zeitschrift für die Alttestamentliche Wissenschaft*
CBC	Cambridge Bible Commentary on the New English Bible, Cambridge
CBQ	*Catholic Biblical Quarterly,* Washington, DC
Ev. Theol.	*Evangelische Theologie,* München
ExpT	*Expository Times,* Edinburgh
ET	English translation
HAT	Handbuch zum Alten Testament, Tübingen
HTR	*Harvard Theological Review,* Cambridge, MA
IB	*Interpreter's Bible,* New York and Nashville
ICC	International Critical Commentary, Edinburgh
ITC	*International Theological Commentary,* Grand Rapids and Edinburgh
JSOT	*Journal for the Study of the Old Testament,* Sheffield
JTS	*Journal of Theological Studies,* Oxford
KAT	Kommentar zum Alten Testament, Gütersloh
LXX	Septuagint (the Greek translation of the Hebrew Bible)
MT	Masoretic Text (the received text of the Hebrew Bible)
NCB	New Century Bible, London
NEB	New English Bible

NICOT	The New International Critical Commentary on the Old Testament, Grand Rapids and London
OTL	Old Testament Library, London and Philadelphia
RHPR	*Revue d'histoire et de philosophie religieuses*, Strasbourg
RSV	Revised Standard Version
SBL	Society of Biblical Literature
SBT	Studies in Biblical Theology, London and Naperville, IL
SVT	Supplements to *Vetus Testamentum*, Leiden
TBC	Torch Bible Commentaries, London
TOTC	Tyndale Old Testament Commentaries, London and Leicester
VT	*Vetus Testamentum*, Leiden
West. Comm.	Westminster Commentaries, London
WMANT	Wissenschaftliche Monographien zum Alten und Neuen Testament, Neukirchen
ZAW	*Zeitschrift für die alttestamentliche Wissenschaft*, Giessen and Berlin
ZDMG	*Zeitschrift der Deutschen Morgenländischen Gesellschaft*, Wiesbaden

ACKNOWLEDGMENT

I am very grateful to Professors Norman Whybray who, as Editor of the series, made very helpful suggestions at an early stage of this book and David J.A. Clines for careful assistance at its proof stage. Neither of course is responsible for the views expressed nor for the limitations and blemishes which remain.

MICAH

Select List of Commentaries

L.C. Allen, *The Books of Joel, Obadiah, Jonah and Micah*, NICOT, 1976. Conservative, but with full, scholarly and well-informed discussion.

D.R. Hillers, *Micah,* Hermeneia, Philadelphia, 1984. Rightly critical of over-detailed redaction criticism. Hillers sees a continuing process of the 'revitalization' of the text behind the present form of the book.

J.L. Mays, *Micah*, OTL, 1976. Deservedly one of the best known commentaries in English, but suffers a little in comparison with the author's commentaries on Amos and Hosea by a strange division of the text and somewhat forced understanding of the purpose of each section.

H. McKeating, *Amos, Hosea, Micah*, CBC, 1971. A commentary which exploits to the full the very limited space offered by this series.

R.L. Smith, *Micah–Malachi*, Word Biblical Commentary, 32, Waco, 1984. A conservative but instructive commentary which takes full note of contemporary scholarship.

D.W. Thomas, 'Micah', *Peake's Commentary on the Bible* (revised edn), ed. M. Black and H.H. Rowley, 1962, pp. 630-34. An outstanding scholar operating in very limited space.

R.E. Wolfe, 'The Book of Micah', *IB,* New York and Nashville, 1956, pp. 897-949. A good 'standard' commentary inevitably now overtaken by a great deal of more recent work.

H.W. Wolff, *Micah the Prophet*, Philadelphia, 1981 (ET of *Mit Micha reden: Prophetie einst und jetzt,* München, 1978). A blend of academic scholarship and 'exposition' relating the message of Micah to modern times.

Commentaries in foreign languages

A. Weiser, *Die Propheten Hosea, Joel, Amos, Obadja, Jona, Micha,* ATD 24, 6th edn, 1985.

B. Renaud, *Michée, Sophonie, Nahum*, Paris, 1987.

R. Vuilleumier and C.A. Keller, *Michée, Nahoum, Habacuc, Sophonie*, Commentaire de l'Ancien Testament, Neuchâtel, 1971.

1

INTRODUCTION

THE STORY IS TOLD of a lady who, beginning to read Shakespeare only late in life, said she was delighted to find him so full of quotations. The reader of the book of Micah, perhaps for many people one of the less familiar of the Old Testament prophets, may have a similar experience. Everyone knows more of it than he or she suspects. It contains one of the finest religious statements of all time:

> 'With what shall I come before the LORD,
> and bow myself before God on high?
> Shall I come before him with burnt offerings,
> with calves a year old?...
> Shall I give my first-born for my transgression,
> the fruit of my body for the sin of my soul?'
> He has showed you, O man, what is good;
> and what does the LORD require of you
> but to do justice, and to love kindness,
> and to walk humbly with your God? (6.6-8).

It is the source of a promise familiar to every Christian reader from the Christmas liturgy:

> But you, O Bethlehem Ephrathah,
> who are little to be among the clans of Judah,
> from you shall come forth for me
> one who is to be ruler in Israel... (5.2 [Heb. 1]).

It shares with the book of Isaiah the promise of God's universal rule in a restored and elevated Jerusalem so that the nations will come there and submit themselves to his adjudication and rule. As a result,

> ... they shall beat their swords into plowshares,
> and their spears into pruning hooks;
> nation shall not lift up sword against nation,
> neither shall they learn war any more (4.3).

It evinces just as passionate a concern for justice towards the underdogs of society as any pre-exilic prophet. To the oppressive rulers the word comes:

> Is it not for you to know justice?—
> you who hate the good and love the evil
> who tear the skin from off my people . . .
> and flay their skin from off them,
> and break their bones in pieces,
> and chop them up like meat in a kettle,
> like flesh in a cauldron (3.1-).

In other words, they not only 'devour' the poor but make a sacrifice of them, sacrificing to their own ends those to whose service they were called as 'shepherds'.

At the end of the book is one of the clearest Old Testament expressions of faith in God as a God of grace:

> Who is a God like thee, pardoning iniquity
> and passing over transgression...?
> He does not retain his anger for ever
> because he delights in steadfast love (7.18).

To engage in study of the book of Micah is not to embark on a journey into entirely unfamiliar territory and it is certainly not a journey without rewards for the traveller.

2

THE CONTENTS
OF THE BOOK

B EFORE DISCUSSING the book in detail and considering
the questions it raises for interpretation it will be useful to
have a map of its contents before us. Even drawing the main
outlines of the shape of the book raises big questions about its
structure, questions which, as we shall see, have found very
different answers. At this stage, however, we may risk begging
many of these issues by giving an outline which has often been
accepted.

1. Chapters 1–3. Mainly oracles of judgment against Samaria and Judah

1.1   Heading (or Superscription).

1.2-7   An oracle against Samaria culminating in a prediction of the reduction of the city to ruins. Verse 5cd extends the scope of the oracle to include Judah and Jerusalem while v. 2 sets it on a universal scale.

1.8-16   An oracle of judgment against Judah and Jerusalem in the form of a lament by the prophet as he sees an invading army advancing. It is marked by considerable word-play on the names of the places mentioned.

2.1-5   A 'woe' oracle against 'this family', announcing judgment by military defeat because of the social and economic oppression of the weak by the powerful and wealthy.

2.6-11   A controversy between Micah and his opponents.

2.12-13   An (apparent) oracle of salvation for Jacob/Israel.

3.1-12   Oracles of judgment against
           (a)   the ruling classes (vv. 1-4)
           (b)   the prophets (vv. 5-8)

(c)　the ruling classes, including priests and prophets, culminating in the threat of the total destruction of Jerusalem (vv. 9-12).

2. Chapter 4–5. Oracles of salvation

(N.B. Alternative verse references here and in the remainder of this book are those of the Hebrew text where it differs from the numbering in the English translations.)

4.1-4	An oracle promising the universal rule of Yahweh in a restored and elevated Jerusalem (= Isa. 2.2-4).
4.5	An addition, urging Israelite loyalty to Yahweh.
4.6-7	Yahweh, as universal king, will bring back the dispersed 'remnant'.
4.8–5.1 [4.14]	The deliverance of Jerusalem from the assault of the nations.
5.2-4 [1-3]	The promise of a new ruler from Bethlehem.
5.5-9 [4-8]	A further promise of military deliverance for the remnant.
5.10-15 [9-14]	Renewal and cleansing for the people of God from all religious syncretism and false trust in military might.

3. Chapters 6–7. Further oracles of judgment and hope

6.1-8	A legal dispute (Heb. *rîb*) between Yahweh and his people calling for justice and loyalty to the covenant.
6.9-16	An announcement by Yahweh that he will destroy 'the city' by famine and invasion because of its social and economic injustice.
7.1-7	The lament of an individual for the evil state of society. The 'I' may be a representative figure. The passage may belong with
7.8-20	A 'prophetic liturgy' pleading for and announcing God's deliverance of his people.

If this table of contents is likened to a map, it is a very small-scale map and, as such, lacks precision and detail. It is by no means always clear where one section ends and another begins; and to make decisions about such divisions is already to have begun to make decisions about interpretation. A number of commentators have divided the final form of the book differently from the outline given above. Later we shall describe and discuss the method of study by which they have made deductions about the process of the 'shaping' of the book, a method often known as 'Redaction Criticism'; but it may be convenient here to mention some of the results to which they have come.

J.L. Mays (1976) believed that in its final form the book is arranged in two parts, chs. 1–5 and chs. 6–7 Each of these is introduced by the summons 'Hear!' (1.2 and 6.1), and each is 'arranged so as to unfold a revelation of YHWH's way in the world' (p. 3). The address of the first part is a universal one, to 'all people', while in the second Israel alone is addressed. But this is, perhaps, the least satisfactory of the arrangements proposed. The summons 'Hear!' appears several times throughout the book (e.g. 3.1, 9; 6.1, 2, 9). Hagstrom (1988), who shares Mays's division of the book, has to admit that the significance of the summons 'Hear!' as a 'structural indicator in the book of Micah . . . must be carefully qualified' (p. 128). Moreover 'YHWH's way in the world' is a very general phrase to describe the contents of a body of prophetic material and, while 1.2 certainly extends the address of, at least, the first oracle onto a universal scale, there is just as much which affects Israel in chs. 1–5 as there is in chs. 6-7 (e.g. 1.4-7, 8-16; 2.1-11 [notice the address 'O house of Jacob' in v. 7]; 2.12f.; 3.1-12 [again with the address, 'Hear, you heads of Jacob']). Further, this division underemphasizes the very disparate material within chs. 1–5. Another scholar who divided the book into the same two parts was Lescow (1972).

Others have found a four-fold division more appropriate, i.e. chs. 1–3, 4–5, 6.1–7.6 and 7.7-20 (or 8-20). This gives a twice repeated 'Judgment–Salvation' pattern, judgment being the theme of chs. 1–3, salvation of chs. 4–5, judgment again in 6.1–7.6 and salvation in 7.7-20 (so, e.g., Fohrer [1968/70], pp. 444-47). Willi-Plein (1971) also saw a four-fold division, but a different one, each section being introduced by the imperative 'Hear!' in 1.2; 3.1; 3.9; 6.2. Yet others have argued for a three-fold division, but a different one from that outlined above. Willis (1969) found three sections each beginning with 'Hear!' at 1.2; 3.1; 6.1 and each having a threat of judgment followed by a promise of salvation, although the promise sections are longer in chs. 3–5 than in chs. 1–2 and 6–7.

Such remarkable variations in conclusions remind us that there is inevitably a large element of subjectivity in such approaches to the text, while they raise questions about the validity of the enterprise of looking for such deliberate shaping of the final form of the book. We shall return to this when we discuss redaction criticism and the views of Hagstrom.

Further Reading

G. Fohrer, *Introduction to the Old Testament*, New York, Nashville, 1968, London, 1970.

D.G. Hagstrom, *The Coherence of the Book of Micah*, SBL Dissertation Series 89, Atlanta, 1988.

T. Lescow, 'Redaktionsgeschichtliche Analyse von Micha 1–5', *ZAW* 84 (1972), pp. 46-85.

—'Redaktionsgeschichtliche Analyse von Micha 6–7', *ZAW* 84 (1972), pp. 182-212.

I. Willi-Plein, *Vorformen der Schriftexegese innerhalb des Alten Testaments*, BZAW 123, 1971.

J.T. Willis, 'The Structure of Micah 3–5 and the Functions of Micah 5.9-14', *ZAW* 81 (1969), pp. 191-214.

—'The Authenticity and Meaning of Micah 5.9-14', *ZAW* 81 (1969), pp. 353-68.

3

THE HISTORICAL
BACKGROUND

THE SUPERSCRIPTION IN 1.1 tells us that Micah received and proclaimed oracles relating to Samaria and Jerusalem during the reigns of Jotham, Ahaz and Hezekiah. There is uncertainty about the exact chronology of the kings of Judah at this time (it is hard to get the figures given in the Bible to add up accurately) but a general consensus of opinion would give the following dates:

Jotham	742–735 BCE
Ahaz	735–715 BCE
Hezekiah	715–687 BCE

Most of the prophetic books have such superscriptions. They were not written by the prophets themselves, for no one talks about himself in the third person in such a way. They belong to the later stages of the editing of the book which may have taken place long after the life and ministry of the particular prophet. In some instances information may be faulty or imperfectly remembered. In others, there may be some special ideological reason for locating a prophet's ministry at a particular period. It is often argued, for example, that the claim in Jer. 1.2 that Jeremiah was called in the thirteenth year of Josiah (626 BCE) places him too early, since there is no evidence in the book that he was active before about 609 BCE. Some believe that the editors of the book, supporters of the Deuteronomic laws which were said to have been behind Josiah's religious reformation (621 BCE), wanted to claim Jeremiah as a supporter of those reforms.

Similarly in the book of Micah there is no compelling evidence to locate the prophet's ministry as early as the reign of Jotham. Indeed, some scholars (e.g. R.E. Wolfe) have argued that Micah's oracles fit only the reign of Hezekiah. They say that the oracle in ch. 1 against Samaria is either to be attributed to another prophet of pre-exilic times, or is so late that it refers to the Samaritan schism long after the exile (so Lescow). More generally, the prediction of the fall of Samaria, which took place in 721 BCE, is taken to indicate that the prophet was active in the time of Ahaz (so, for example, D.W. Thomas).

We do not know if there was any ideological reason for extending the period of Micah's ministry back to the reign of Jotham. But its effect was to place the beginning of that ministry in a time of some national insecurity. Jotham's immediate predecessor had been Uzziah who enjoyed a long, secure and prosperous reign of some forty years (783–742 BCE). Many in Judah would have known no other king, and his death would have been read as an end to a settled and safe era. His departure must have appeared to open a door to an uneasy foreboding of change and danger. In some ways it must have struck Judaeans of the eighth century rather as Queen Victoria's death affected many in Britain after her long reign. To make matters worse, Uzziah's death coincided exactly with the beginning of a period of imperial expansion by Assyria. For the whole of the rest of the eighth century the Near East was to be menaced by the shadow of this great and aggressive military power. To live in Judah or Israel at this time must have been rather like living in one of the small Balkan or European states as the shadow of Nazi Germany loomed ever larger and longer during the 1930s. The superscription to the book of Micah, by stretching Micah's ministry back to the reign of Jotham, leaves the reader in no doubt that the major part of the prophet's ministry took place in such a time of threat and insecurity. The chickens of the nation's sin were coming home to roost in judgment. Perhaps the purpose was to claim fresh relevance for the book in some later time of similar despair, danger and uncertainty.

It was Assyrian pressure which led Syria and Israel, under their kings Rezin and Pekah, to form a defensive coalition to resist the threat from that quarter; and they in turn put pressure on Ahaz of Judah to join them. When he (wisely) demurred they invaded Judah in 735 BCE in order to depose him and put a puppet king of their own, Tabe'el (a Syrian name), on the throne to carry out their policy. We read of this in 2 Kgs 16.5, while the added details of Edom's success in freeing itself from Judaean control and the Chronicler's account of a threat from the Philistines (2 Chron. 28.18) at this time suggest a period of great peril for Judah. A more detailed account of the attack and siege of Jerusalem is given in Isa. 7.1-17, which relates how Isaiah confronted Ahaz as he was preparing Jerusalem's defences. The prophet called on the king to have faith in God rather than follow a policy of political expediency in allying himself with other powers. This incident reminds us that Micah and Isaiah must have been contemporaries, although there is no mention of one by the other. Both apparently delivered similar messages, especially in denouncing the greed and ruthlessness of the powerful and wealthy, in predicting judgment from God, and in calling for ethical righteousness in society. The oracle common to both books (Mic. 4.1-4 = Isa. 2.2-4, with an additional verse in Micah) is, however no evidence of collaboration; its appearance in both books must be taken as evidence of a later stage of redaction of the two collections.

In fact Ahaz appealed to Tiglath-pileser of Assyria for help and apparently obtained it, for the Syro-Ephraimite invasion did not succeed. However there was a considerable price to pay, for Ahaz became a political vassal of Assyria. Since this would probably have happened in any case, Ahaz's voluntary submission to that power could perhaps be regarded as astuteness on his part. This policy kept Judah in a state of uneasy peace while affairs deteriorated sharply for the northern kingdom of Israel. As a consequence of repeated unwise alliances against Assyria, the territory and independence of the north were steadily eroded. The final blow came in 721 BCE when Samaria was captured by the Assyrian king Shalmaneser, although its final destruction was apparently carried out by his successor, Sargon II. Mic. 1.6f. appears to predict this event, while in v. 5b a later editor has reflected on the incident as a just punishment for Israel's sin and has added a

Micah

reference to Judah to show that it was equally guilty. The episode naturally made a deep impression on the south. Not only does Isaiah utter threats of judgment against Samaria (e.g. Isa. 8.4), but the editors of the books of Kings pause for a long theological reflection on the disaster when they reach this point in their story (2 Kgs 17.7-18).

It was in the time of Ahaz's son and successor, Hezekiah, that Judah suffered the gravest threats from Assyria. In 712 BCE Sargon marched west to deal with another coalition organized against him by Egypt, Philistia and Phoenicia, into which Hezekiah had been inveigled. Isaiah bitterly opposed this venture; his words and symbolic acts denouncing it are recorded in Isaiah 20, culminating in an impassioned warning of the disaster to come if Hezekiah persisted: 'And we, how shall we escape?' (v. 6).

Hezekiah himself seems to have promoted strongly the cause of Yahwism, no doubt partly from the political motives of strengthening and uniting the kingdom under his power; he may even have hoped to bring the people of the old northern kingdom once again under the rule of the Davidic dynasty. He also made energetic efforts to improve the city's defences; present-day visitors to Jerusalem may still see preserved part of the massive wall he had constructed to enclose not only the old city but a wider area to the west. He also had the famous Siloam tunnel constructed to improve the city's water supplies under siege.

Perhaps all this bred false confidence. In the belief that internal troubles in the Assyrian empire offered an opportunity to strike for independence, a great coalition of states sprang up determined to break Assyrian rule, including the old allies: Egypt, Phoenicia and the cities of Philistia. Hezekiah brought Judah uncompromisingly into the alliance. His seems almost to have been a ringleader's role for, when the king of Ekron refused to join the allies (rather like Ahaz earlier), he was deposed, and Hezekiah took him into custody in Jerusalem.

The hopes of this coalition were as short-lived as those of its predecessors. In a series of reprisal raids between 703 and 701 BCE Sennacherib launched the Assyrian army against the members of the alliance, overrunning each in turn. In 701 he marched into Judah, capturing and destroying many of its major cities, whose inhabitants he brutally punished. Jerusalem itself was besieged but not captured; it is not entirely clear why this was so. 2 Kgs 18.13-16 and Assyrian inscriptions tell of the payment of a large amount of tribute by Hezekiah by which he 'bought off' Sennacherib. In later times, however, the episode was remembered as a miraculous deliverance of the city by God, fulfilling the promises solemnly proclaimed in the worship in the Temple (e.g. Pss. 132.13f.; 46; 48). The narrative of 2 Kgs 18.17–19.37 combines at least two further accounts of the whole incident, both of which interpret it as a direct intervention by God. Whatever exactly occurred, the consequence was that Judah lost independence for many years and, after Hezekiah's death, his son Manasseh remained subject to Assyrian control throughout his long reign.

These, then, were the major political events which formed the backdrop to Micah's ministry. Both his words and those of his contemporary, Isaiah, make clear that some of the same social abuses which Amos and Hosea had denounced in the northern kingdom flourished in Judah. Extreme wealth for some led to exploitation and oppression of the poorer peasants and smallholders. Micah is not specific, but a charge like that in 2.1f., taken together with the more definite words of Amos, suggests that wealthy capitalists lent money at high rates of interest and mercilessly foreclosed on the mortgage of any who, perhaps because of a bad harvest one year, could not pay by settlement date. 3.1-3 suggests there was little hope for the weak and the poor of getting redress in the courts. Those who should have been establishing and preserving 'justice' in the land did not act as though they even knew what it was. On the contrary, rulers and priests abused their power at the expense of the 'small' people in Judah. Meanwhile, many of the prophets of the official cultic worship proved toothless tigers, not wanting to offend those who paid them well (3.5).

Anyone who threatened to disturb this happy state of profitable compromise was not likely to be welcome, and Micah appears to have run into as much opposition as any prophet of Old Testament times (2.6-11). They were certainly tumultuous days in which to be called to be one of Yahweh's prophets in Judah.

Further Reading

J. Bright, *A History of Israel*, London, 3rd edn, 1980.

B.S. Childs, *Isaiah and the Assyrian Crisis*, SBT II/3, London, 1967.

R.E. Clements, *Isaiah and the Deliverance of Jerusalem*, JSOTS 13, Sheffield, 1980.

ḋ. Donner, 'The Separate States of Israel and Judah', *Israelite and Judaean History*, ed. J.H. Hayes and J.M. Miller, OTL, London, 1977, esp. pp. 415-34.

J.W. McKay, *Religion in Judah under the Assyrians*, SBT II/26, London, 1973.

B. Oded, 'Judah and the Exile', *in Israelite and Judaean History*, ed. J.H. Hayes and J.M. Miller, OTL, London, 1977, esp. pp. 435-57.

H.H. Rowley, 'Hezekiah's Reform and Rebellion', *BJRL* 44 (1961-62), pp. 395-461 = *Men of God*, London, 1963, pp. 98-132.

D.W. Thomas, 'Micah', *Peake's Commentary on the Bible*, pp. 630-34.

R.E. Wolfe, 'The Book of Micah', *IB* pp. 897-949.

4

MICAH
THE MAN

W E KNOW VERY LITTLE about Micah as a person. We are told in the superscription (1.1) and in Jer. 26.18 that he was a 'Moreshite', that is, he was a native of Moresheth, probably the small town of Moresheth-gath mentioned in 1.14. This is usually identified with modern Tell el-Judeideh, about 25 miles south-west of Jerusalem on the edge of the 'Shephelah', the low hill range which rises up from the coastal plain towards the central heights. Modern visitors to Jerusalem traverse it after leaving Tel Aviv airport. The town was probably at one time a dependent settlement of Gath, the Philistian city, but in the eighth century it was one of the fortified towns defending the south-western approaches to Judah and, above all, to Jerusalem. It is often pointed out that people are only called by the name of the place they come from when living elsewhere. For example, the Spaniards called one of their great painters, *El Greco*, for it was the fact that he was a Greek which struck them most forcefully. So, perhaps, Micah came to Jerusalem and stayed there, preaching and teaching, and so was known as 'the Moreshite'.

Whereas Isaiah is often said to have belonged to the upper classes, since he had access to the king and mixed with leading priests and other officials, Micah appears to have known about oppression from the bottom of the heap. He knew exactly how the overbearing policies of the leaders bore down on the day-to-day life of ordinary peasants, and his attacks are all against what today we should call the political and religious 'Establishment' (e.g. 3.1-3, 9-12). It is the policies of these groups he attacks, not the ordinary people—that is, on the assumption that the charges of general religious apostasy and syncretism in the book belong to later stages of its formation (e.g. 1.7; 5.10-16; 6.16). This may mean that Micah came from the peasant classes and was horrified by what he saw in his own district and in Jerusalem. Perhaps it was such a sense of outrage which he understood to be God's call to prophesy against the leaders in the land, rather as the later Jeremiah seems to have been appalled by what he saw when he moved from the village of Anathoth to the city (Jer. 5.1-5).

But was Micah a prophet at all? He is not called such, although the superscription brings him into line with similar editorial notes about Amos (Amos 1.1) and Isaiah (Isa. 1.1; 2.1; 13.1; etc.). Wolff (1977) argued that Micah was not a prophet. Rather, he was an elder from Moresheth, one of those responsible for administering true justice in the community. He pointed out that there is no account of a prophetic call of Micah. Only rarely does Micah use prophetic formulae to introduce or conclude oracles. These appear only at 2.3 ('Therefore, thus says the LORD') and 3.5 ('Thus says the LORD concerning the prophets'); and there they may be redactional additions. In fact, God is usually only named when Micah is quoting his opponents (2.7; 3.4, 11). His name is strangely absent, for example, from 3.12, the climax of Micah's pronouncements against the leaders of the city. In 3.8 also, apart from the phrase 'the Spirit of the LORD', often seen as an addition, there is nothing of Yahweh. The 'And I said' of 3.1 is in contrast to the words of the false prophets and is somewhat akin to the use of the first person 'I' by Wisdom in Proverbs 8 and Sir. 24.1. It is a remnant also of the old clan wisdom style (Prov. 8.12, 14, 20, etc.). Micah does not use the term 'king' but rather the title 'heads', descriptive of the heads of the old clans, and 'rulers', used of the 'judges'. His concern is above all for 'justice'. All of this suggests, according to Wolff, that Micah himself was one of the clan elders who were guardians of the 'wisdom' tradition and who were responsible for administering justice in the community. It was because he saw the leaders in Jerusalem failing to maintain this responsibility towards the ordinary people in the Judaean countryside that he went to the city to challenge them.

This view has not been widely adopted. Carrera (1982) agreed with Wolff that Micah belonged in the stream of Old Testament wisdom, but Weiser places Micah firmly among the prophets (1985, p. 230) as does van der Woude (1982, p. 49), who specifically rejects Wolff's arguments. Wolff was writing at a time when scholars were tending to find 'Wisdom' traditions everywhere, whereas today we should be more cautious about claiming to establish close links between a particular prophet and the wisdom teachers. Perhaps also we might be less sure that village 'elders' were the guardians of such wisdom traditions. Further, it is clear, both from the present form of the book as well as from Jer. 26.16-20, where it is specifically stated that Micah had 'prophesied', that tradition remembered him as a prophet. The unusual form of Micah's 'prophecies' should be noted; but this may only serve to remind us that Micah did not belong to the 'mainstream' of Old Testament prophets, and that Old Testament prophecy was a very varied phenomenon. Wolff's argument does, however, have the value of underlining the truth that Old Testament prophets were passionately concerned with justice in society. Whatever else Micah may or may not have been, he was clearly aflame with a sense of burning indignation at the unjust system in which so many ordinary people suffered at the hands of the powerful and wealthy. He is the 'Piers Plowman' of the Old Testament. He seems to have been more a prophet of the market place and the town square than the sanctuary. For him, Yahwism was nothing if it did not affect the political and social life of society. He apparently set little store by the great 'institutions' of the nation and its religion, whether that meant temple, palace or 'chosen city'. God could and would dispense with all of these if necessary (3.12); and this, if the passage comes from him, is also the implication of 6.6-8. If Micah did see any hope beyond such a total catastrophe as he believed was coming on nation and temple, it must have been a future with a new set of institutions and a new line of leaders.

At least his preaching must have made an impression. It was remembered nearly one hundred years later (Jer. 26.16-19). Micah is the only Old Testament prophet to be mentioned by name in another prophetic book (unless we include the mention of Jeremiah in the book of Daniel, which is in fact not a prophetic book). Further, the argument will be put forward here that his preaching became, in a special way, the 'text' for exposition after the exile.

Further Reading

J.N. Carrera, 'Kunstsprache und Weisheit bei Micha', *BZ* 26 (1982), pp. 50-74.

H.W. Wolff, 'Wie verstand Micha von Moresheth sein prophetisches Amt?', *SVT* 29 (1977), pp. 403-17.

A.S. van der Woude, 'Three Classical Prophets', *in Israel's Prophetic Tradition*, ed. R.J. Coggins and others, Cambridge, 1982, pp. 32-57.

5

THE HISTORY
OF CRITICISM

FOR MORE THAN A HUNDRED years the small book of Micah
has been a critical battlefield. The main points at issue have
been (i) how much of the present book comes from Micah
himself? and (ii) how did the book achieve its present form?
Both questions bring a number of others with them. On what
principles was additional material brought in? What theological and exegetical function was the final shaping process
intended to serve? Can we date various stages in its evolution?
Generally speaking, the attempt to answer the first question
about the authorship of various elements in the book involved
the use of 'literary-critical' methods. Literary, historical and
theological criteria were used in order to determine what was
original to the prophet and what came from other and later
hands. The second question, which is more concerned with the
present shape of the book, has involved the use of form- and
redaction-critical methods. It has led to the search for and
examination of the various traditions and points of view represented in different strata in the book. Naturally, the questions
are inter-related and the methods of investigation used to
answer them overlap. It would be wrong to suggest that the
literary-critical and form- and redaction-critical methods
simply succeeded one another chronologically. Literary critics
have raised theological issues, and critics examining the final
form of the book have continued to make judgments on the
basis of what they think does, and does not, come from Micah.
Nevertheless, it is true to say that interest in the stages of the
book's growth and in the purposes of those responsible for each

editorial layer has predominated in more recent study. Earlier scholars sometimes seemed almost dismissive of the value of later additions or 'accretions' to the original words of the historical Micah. It was as though they saw their work to be like that of cleaning an old painting, stripping off the deposit of centuries in order to get back to the 'authentic' colours of the original message. Their vocabulary is revealing. They often spoke of what was 'genuine' or 'authentic', implying that all later additions was somehow counterfeit. Too often they seem to have assumed that 'gloss' equals 'dross'. More recently scholars have seen in the late material valuable evidence for the ways in which the teaching of a prophet was handed down, re-interpreted and re-applied in new situations. The book as we have it is a witness to the living tradition as it was preserved in the continuing communities of faith, and witness also to the power of the original word to go on addressing later generations with new vitality and relevance. To use a different image, modern study of a prophetic book is something like the work of an archaeologist investigating an ancient mound (a *tell*). Starting with what we now have we dig down to discover layer upon layer, each being the deposit of a different generation of inhabitants and each revealing something about these and their development.

(i) *Literary Criticism*

It was Heinrich Ewald who first began to question Micah's authorship of the whole book. Between the first and second editions of his study of the prophets (*Die Propheten des Alten Bundes*, 1840, 1867), he changed his mind about the integrity of the whole. He pointed out that while chs. 1–5 remain complete in themselves, the style of chs. 6–7 is varied. These two chapters form a dramatic poem in which different voices speak. The religious abuses they describe reflect the time of Manasseh (7th century BCE, and so the century after Micah). In 1878, J. Wellhausen followed Ewald in his dating of 6.1–7.6 to the time of Manasseh but said that 7.7-20 showed parallels with Second Isaiah (Isa. 40–55) and so was exilic in date. The most influential contribution in that period, however, was that of B. Stade, in an article which is still referred to in almost every commentary on Micah (*ZAW* 1 [1881], pp. 161-72). In it he argued that only in chs. 1–3 do we hear Micah's own words (with the exception of 2.12f.). 1.2-16 announces coming judgment from Yahweh on Judah and Samaria. Chapters 2–3 (with the exception of 2.12f.) show a similar recurring pattern: description of sins (2.1f., 8-10; 3.2, 9-11); announcement of judgment (2.3-5; 3.6); the people's response (2.6, 11); and the prophet's reply (2.7; 3.7f.). The sins described fit the time of Ahaz and Hezekiah especially as they are described in the book of Isaiah; and Stade draws on no fewer than twenty-one Isaianic passages which he sees as having parallels in Micah. (Hitzig, however, had shown that for 2.12f. the real parallels were to be found in Jeremiah and Second Isaiah, with none at all in Isaiah 1–39.) Since these verses break the structure that he found in chs. 2–3, which required an announcement of judgment at this stage, they are clearly later. In parallels with chs. 4–5, Ezekiel and Second Isaiah and other post-exilic prophets indicate that these chapters also are post-exilic. Certainly the conditions reflected in such passages as 4.11f. reflect the time of the exile, while 5.2f. comes from a time after the historical line of Davidic kings had come to an end. Later (*Geschichte des Volkes Israel*, I, 1887, p. 634), Stade went on to argue that ch. 6 also is post-exilic. He also made a point which has been repeated many times: the reference to Micah in Jer. 26.17ff. shows that the historic prophet was remembered only as a messenger of judgment.

Stade was also one of the few early critics denying any message of hope to Micah who faced the question, 'If Micah preached only judgment, how and why were the oracles of salvation added to his work?' His answer (*ZAW* 23 [1903], pp. 163-71) was that the one-sided nature of Micah's message of total destruction was only partially fulfilled. His gloom was in stark contrast to the messianic hope of Isaiah and to the optimism which is shown in the books of Habakkuk and Nahum. To find canonical acceptance the book of Micah also needed such an element, so, once prophecy had ceased after the exile, scribes added to the book an imitation of prophetic oracles expressing future hope. In some ways this approach has a 'modern' ring about it, as also does another suggestion of Stade's that 7.7-20 is to be viewed as a psalm coming from the post-exilic community. The 'I' here is not the prophet but the community (indeed, the passage is not prophecy at all: it is lyric poetry). This is often the case in the Psalms, where also the 'I' can change easily to 'we' (cf. vv. 19f.). In the same article Stade argued that 1.2-4 is post-exilic, reflecting the coming of Yahweh for world judgment, a concept peculiar to late, post-exilic prophecy and apocalyptic (pp. 153-71).

Stade's work was so seminal that already before it was completed the main lines of much subsequent discussion had been laid down. How could one and the same prophet announce the apparently total judgment of 3.12 and yet hold out the hopes expressed in chs. 4–5 and 7.7-20? Language, theology, and the nature of the eschatological hopes expressed there seemed to many to parallel exilic and post-exilic prophecy, while ch. 5 apparently assumed that the Davidic line no longer ruled in Jerusalem. Whereas in the first three chapters Micah attacked the social evils of oppression and injustice tolerated, or even caused, by the leadership of the community, elsewhere the sins of cultic apostasy of the whole nation were held to be responsible for judgment, an apostasy described (e.g. in 5.12-15 and 6.16) in terms very reminiscent of much of the 'Deuteronomistic' literature of later prophecy (e.g. 5.10f.).

It would be tedious to follow every commentator's analysis of what is, and what is not, from Micah and the detailed reasons of each for making the distinction. Stade's influence is seen everywhere. J.M.P. Smith (1911), who gave a remarkably full survey of the history of criticism to that time, asserted that one can know of Micah only that which can be gleaned from chs. 1–3. While it is possible that 6.9-16 and 7.1-6 are from him, chs. 6–7 are 'a collection of miscellaneous fragments from widely scattered periods and from at least four different authors' (p. 16). H.W. Robinson could discern Micah's authority with certainly only in chs. 1–3 (always excepting 2.12f.); and, while 6.1–7.6 could be by Micah, the probability was that these are 'anonymous prophecies', written somewhat after those of Micah and rightly felt to be not unlike his in theme. They were added 'at a much later date' (Westminster Commentaries, 1919, p. 559). Similar views were expressed by G.W. Wade and T.H. Robinson (1964). R.E. Wolfe (1956) held that 6.1–7.4 could have contained Micah's own oracles, but that otherwise his words are found only in chs. 1–3 (excepting 1.2-4 and 2.12f.). D.W. Thomas (1962) saw Micah's hand in chs. 1–3, while of 6.1–7.4, '6.6–7.4 is most likely to be his work'. Mays (1976) is among the most radical of modern commentators. He finds Micah's words only in 1.3-5a, 8-15; 2.1-5, 6-11; 3.1-4, 5-8 and 9-12. Even in these passages there have been editorial revisions and additions. Like many others, Mays sees the reference to 'the Spirit of Yahweh' in 3.8 as additional. Another scholar who combines a strong homiletical interest in Micah with a radical view of the amount of redactional elements in the book is Wolff (1981). He claims only 1.8-16, 2.1-11 and 3.1-12 as certainly coming from Micah, although his hand can be seen also to some extent in 1.6f., 4.9–5.3(2) and in 6.9-16, 'albeit in a precarious state of preservation' (p. 17).

For these and many other commentators Wolfe speaks when he says, 'In a sense Micah is a source book for observing the development of Hebrew thought from 714 BC to approximately 200 BC' (1956, p. 900).

However, not all the more recent commentators have been so pessimistic about our ability to trace Micah's own mind in much of the material we have. As long ago as 1922 E. Sellin, (*Das Zwölfprophetenbuch*, KAT), while recognizing the controversy surrounding 2.12f., 4.1-5 and 6.1–7.6 and acknowledging later elements in them, did not find compelling reasons for denying their authenticity entirely, although he did allow for some dislocation of their original order (p. 260). Nor did the very different tone of 6.1–7.6 necessarily imply a different author. This could be explained by seeing this passage as coming from a different period in Micah's own lifetime. More recently, as is perhaps to be expected, a conservative commentator, B.K. Waltke (1988) has concluded that '...there is no compelling reason to urge against the authenticity of any oracle in Micah' (p. 149). Similarly L.C. Allen (1976) writes, 'It is possible...to defend the Mican origin of most of the book apart from 4.1-4 [the oracle common to the books of Micah and Isaiah which Allen sees as earlier than both of them], 4.6-8 and 7.8-20' (p. 251). Waltke sees this as an example of Allen's 'bowing' to the opinion of other scholars but offering 'no evidence to validate his scepticism'!

What is more surprising is that a scholar such as A. Weiser, (1985) assigns to Micah, not only ch. 1 (with the exception of v. 5b), 2.1-11 and ch. 3, but possibly also 5.1-5, 9-14; 6.1-8, 9-16 and 7.1-7. 7.8-20 he believes to be a prophetic liturgy from a later time; but 'the attempt which is often made to deny all the oracles in chs. 4–7 to Micah and to see the promises as a post-exilic collection is not necessary, since the double transition of warning and promise only finds sufficient explanation if one or the other of the promises in chs. 4–5 goes back to Micah himself (p. 232). Weiser agrees that while 4.6-8, 9-13 and 14, which speak of the return of the Diaspora (the term for all dispersed Jews living away from their homeland after the exile), cannot be from the time of Micah, they 'must be considered as a subsequent working over of a genuine word of Micah' (p. 231). Similarly Rudolph (1975) sees only 4.1-4; 5.6-8 and 7.8-20 as additions to Micah's own words.

This raises an important point which seems to have been considered first by A. Kuenen, who said that some of the differences between chs. 1–3 and 4–5 could be explained by the fact that chs. 1–3 dealt with the godless leaders while chs. 4–5 were addressed to the people as a whole (*Theologisch Tijdschrift* 6 [1872], pp. 285-302). This is a contribution to the Micah debate which has been strangely neglected. J.M.P. Smith (ICC, 1911 edn) maintains that no authentic oracle of hope of Micah's is recorded, but nevertheless adds, ' There is no evidence that he looked for the annihilation of the nation as such. Living apart from the glamour and power of the capital *he did not identify the fate of the nation with that of Jerusalem*' (p. 25, italics mine). Micah's attacks were indeed against the religious and political leaders, the 'Establishment' of Judah. It is by no means unlikely that he saw some future purpose of God for the people, and that such an expression of hope furnished the basis of its later application to the theme of the return of the exiles from Babylon. Nor is it impossible that Micah saw God as dispensing with the present dynasty and starting again with a new 'David' (5.1-4). Such hopes would parallel those in Isa. 9.2-7 and 11.1-9. Our constant frustration is that we cannot date any of these passages with precision. It is one thing to say that it is not impossible that words of Micah lie behind the present oracles of hope in the book (and too many have dismissed that possibility too quickly). It is quite another to prove such an assertion.

One interesting attempt to face the apparent contradictions between the threats of judgment and some of the promises of hope is that made by A.S. van der Woude (1976, pp. 61ff.; 1982, pp. 49ff.). He believes that chs. 1–5 are essentially authentic and that chs. 2–5 record both sides of 'a discussion between Micah and his opponents'. According to van der Woude the difficult 2.12f., which has been seen by so many to intrude a discordant note of hope into the solemn judgment themes of chs. 1–3, actually expresses the words of Micah's opponents, the 'false prophets', members of the royal and temple establishment who, as another prophet said, prophesy ' "Peace" where there is no peace' (Jer. 6.14) or who, in Micah's words, give favourable oracles to those who pay them well but threaten those who do not with the divine displeasure (3.6). 2.12f. furnishes an example of their shallow assurance of God's favour to a society which is corrupt. Chapter 2 opens with Micah's threats, to which his opponents reply by calling on him to be quiet (v. 6), just as Amaziah tried to silence Amos (Amos 7.12f.). Micah replies in vv. 7-11, but their rejoinder to him is a 'stock' 'oracle' of salvation (vv. 12f.). Micah replies again in ch. 3.2 with the contrasting 'But I said' (v. 1), and strongly contrasts his call and authority with theirs (v. 8). The opponents' words are found again in 4.1-5, 6f., 8, 9, 11-13; 5.5f. [4f.], 8f. [7f.]. Micah's answering and correcting oracles are found in 5.1-4 [4.14–5.4] and v. 7 [6]. It is not necessary here to follow van der Woude's view that chs. 6–7 come from a northern prophet of the time of Hosea (he even surmises that this prophet may also have been called Micah!) and that 5.10-15 [9-14] form a Deuteronomistic link between the two. It must be said that his explanation for the whole of the 'hope' element in chs. 4–5 does not carry conviction. That there was controversy between Micah and some who challenged him is clear. What is far from clear is that all the oracles of hope which appear in these chapters should be taken as false prophecy.

One more attempt to deal with 2.12f. may be mentioned. Already in 1924 W.E. Barnes, in a review of a study by Karl Budde on Micah 2–3, argued that 2.12f. is not a promise but a

threat (*JTS* 25 [1924], pp. 81-84). He criticized Budde for following Wellhausen in saying that this is an exilic passage
promising restoration to the exiles in Babylon. Yahweh
'gathers' both his own people and others for judgment as well
as for salvation and protection (as, e.g., in Ps. 50.5; Isa. 24.22);
and, in Mic. 2.12f., 'I will put them together as sheep in a fold'
suggests detention rather than greater freedom. An enemy is
besieging the city as punishment from Yahweh for the sins
described in vv. 1-9. The context also suggests that punishment is in mind, for 'Arise and go! This is no place to rest'
(v. 10) indicates exile. More recently Gershon Brin renewed
this argument (1989). He too points to the judgment contexts
in which the verb 'to gather' is used. The unit beginning in
vv. 6-11 describes the sins of the people but, without vv. 12f., it
lacks a pronouncement of judgment in the usual pattern of
these chapters (others have attributed this to the displacement
of the oracle from an original context in ch. 4). The picture of
the 'sheep' emphasizes Israel's helplessness, and v. 13 suggests
the breaking down of the walls of Jerusalem by an enemy who
then takes the 'sheep' (the people), now defenceless, out into
exile. It should be said that this is not an obvious reading of
2.12f. However, J.L. Mays (1976, pp. 75f.) says that it is v. 13
which has the effect of turning what was an exilic promise of
restoration into an explanation of the truth that the destruction of Jerusalem and the exile are the work of Yahweh. This
fits Mays's belief that the whole book has been edited in two
parts, the first of which, chs. 1–5, shows that Israel's history
from the fall of Samaria and Jerusalem, through the exile, to
the restoration of Zion, revealed Yahweh's strategy for establishing his world reign. If one begins without such a prior
assumption, however, it seems to make more sense to see 2.12
as the later addition, turning what was an original threat of
judgment (v. 13) into a post-exilic promise of restoration.

(ii) *Form and Redaction Criticism*

Obviously commentators can go on discussing precisely which
passages in the book of Micah may be later and which may be
attributed to the prophet. The fact that reputable scholars can
hold such different views reminds us that our tools lack precision. We can be sure that additions have been made. We can-

not always be sure just what those additions are. Perhaps it has been the sense of running into a dead end that has led some scholars to change direction a little. Building on the results of literary criticism rather than abandoning them, these scholars have nevertheless felt it more profitable to ask, 'By what means and for what purposes has the book reached its present form?' 'What can be deduced from that final form of the methods and intentions of those who have selected and ordered the units of material in just the way they have?' Since these are known as 'editors' or 'redactors' of the material this line of enquiry has been called 'redaction criticism'. 'Form criticism' has also seemed to offer an attractive way forward. This involves the study of the type, shape and form of the smaller units of material in the book, the history of their development, their use and the part they played in the life of the community. Both these methods of study have the effect of directing the main attention away from purely *literary* concerns to thoughts about the community which the material served and which produced it.

H. Gunkel, whose pioneer work on form criticism has left such a mark on the study of the Psalms and the Pentateuch, was something of a trail-blazer in Micah studies as well. In 1924 he published an article which subsequently appeared in English ('The Close of Micah', 1928) in which he argued that the whole of 7.7-20 is 'an artistically constructed unit' in four parts. Verses 7-10 form a lament of Zion, personified as feminine in the enemy's gloating in v. 10, in which, as in so many of the psalms of lament, an individual speaks on behalf of the community; vv. 11-13 is an answering divine oracle addressed to Zion; vv. 14-17 is a communal (national) lament 'suffused with the prophetical spirit', and vv. 18-20 a hymn of assurance of future deliverance, marked by the use of the participial clauses so often found in hymns elsewhere in the Old Testament. This approach (which, as we have seen, had been anticipated by Stade) was taken farther by Bo Reicke (1967, pp. 349-67). He included 7.1-6 in the discussion, and argued that the whole chapter should be seen as a liturgical text (p. 350). Verses 1-6 are the words of a representative prophet who speaks on behalf of the community. Neither Gunkel nor Reicke claimed that the prophet was Micah, or even that his identity could be known at all. Both saw the passage as playing a part in the life and worship of the nation, and so directed attention away from literary issues of authorship and historical context towards the function of the material and the nature of the community in which it served this purpose.

This was the same direction as that later taken by the redaction critics. Here we can mention only some of the best known and most influential of them as examples of the method and the results it claims. Behind their conclusions lies an intense and detailed examination of the text which can only be appreciated by a careful reading of their work.

J. Jeremias (1971) believed that additions to Micah's oracles of judgment began to be made in the early period of the exile. These reflect the situation of an exiled community which needed to see the exile as a divine judgment for the sins of the people. Even the oracles of hope, like those of Second Isaiah, reflect the background of that situation of distress. So 1.5b extended Micah's early oracle against Samaria to include Judah, attributing the fall of Jerusalem to comparable sins committed there. Again, 2.3f. extends an original threat of Micah against the leaders of the community in vv. 1f., continued in v. 5, to the 'whole family'. This explains why the judgment of the exile fell on the nation. Similarly, 2.10 takes an attack against Israel's leaders and shows how the whole community could not remain in the land because of their uncleanness. 5.10-14 [9-13] introduces another note not heard from Micah himself, who concentrated on social and legislative injustice. It attacks the community for trusting in other gods and in the power of chariots and horses, and interprets the exile ('in that day', v. 10 [9]) as a means by which Yahweh will root out all such sins. As in Hosea, the exile is believed to have both a punitive and a cleansing effect. Jeremias understands the exegetical methods of the later editing to include the extension of the term 'Israel' to embrace Judah as well. Jeremias is not trying to 'restore' Micah's 'authentic' words in an exercise which is an end in itself. His intention is to direct attention to the exegetical methods and aims of those who added to his words and set them in new contexts.

A much more systematic and detailed examination of some Old Testament books along these lines was offered by Willi-

Plein (1971). The rationale of this approach is that 'glosses' express an interpretation of the prophet's original words, and that the whole process of word and interpretation belongs to the growth of the Old Testament as sacred canon. Willi-Plein found Micah's own words only in chs. 1–3 and 6.9-15. 5.10-13 [9-12] and 6.2-8 may be pre-exilic but they are not from Micah since they do not accord with his message. The first literary collection of his oracles was made during the exile when, once all secondary material is removed, four main sections emerge, each introduced by the imperative 'Hear': 1.2–2.11; 3.1-8, 9-12; 6.2-16. The joining of 2.11 to 3.1 by the phrase 'And I said' may perhaps go back to this exilic redactor. A second stage is marked by the addition during the fifth century BCE of exilic and post-exilic oracles which express a 'pre-apocalyptic' hope for the future such as 4.1-7; 5.2-4 [1-3]. (The term 'pre-apocalyptic' when used by such scholars in this context usually refers to anticipation of Yahweh's saving action within this world's history.) However, a much more sharply 'apocalyptic' edition (God's breaking into this world's history from beyond in supernatural action on a cosmic scale) saw the introduction of oracles such as 5.5-6 [4-5] and 7.11-17. Striking parallels between these and oracles in the later chapters of Zechariah (chs. 9–14) argue for a fourth-century date for this stage of the book.

In 1972, Lescow published two articles that offered a redaction-critical analysis first of Micah 1–5 and then of 6–7. According to Lescow, the material in 1–5 developed in five stages: (i) the primary message of the prophet preserved in chs. 1–3 with its climax in 3.12; (ii) the Zion sayings in ch. 4 (vv. 6f., 8-13) which come from the period of the exile and were drawn from liturgies of lamentation performed on the ruined site of the temple (cf. Jer. 41.4-6; Zech. 7.3f.); (iii) 4.1-4, which reflects the re-founding of the temple. Indeed it may have been this great occasion, which Zechariah said was to transform fasts into joyous festivals (Zech. 8.18f.), which caused chs. 1–3 of Micah to be re-read by the addition of 4.1-4; (iv) the material was next turned into a litany *against* the nations by the addition of apocalyptic passages which make use of the 'war against the nations' theme as in 5.5-15 [4-14]. Such ideas belong to the early years of the fourth century BCE;

(v) the final stage of the book was marked by the addition of 'anti-Samaritan' polemic, found, for example, in 1.6.

Chapters 6–7, according to Lescow, have been compiled on the pattern of what he has called a 'three-stage Torah' (cf. ZAW 82 [1970], pp. 362-79), i.e. (i) the legal dispute of Yahweh against his people in 6.1-8; (ii) the threat of Yahweh's judgment and the people's lament in 6.9-16 and 7.1-6; and (iii) a hymnic liturgy offering assurance of Yahweh's grace in response to repentance in 7.7-20. This addition to the book was occasioned by the Samaritan schism and so has to be dated about 330 BCE. The same 'heresy' is alluded to in 6.16 in the reference to the sins of Omri and Ahab.

A final example of this method is that of B. Renaud (1964, 1977 and his commentary of 1987). Renaud sees four stages in the book's growth. The first took place before the exile. It included words of Micah directed against Samaria before 721 (1.2-7), while the rest of chs. 1–3 was spoken in Judah. It concentrated not on religious apostasy but on social injustice. So chs. 1–3 combined elements of Amos and Hosea, and this is also true of 6.9-15, which also contains original Micah material. The reference to Micah in Jer. 26.18 shows that his words were widely circulated, perhaps among wisdom circles, judges and city councils (a view which carries some echo of Wolff). It is impossible to know if Micah envisages any hope beyond the destruction of Jerusalem, since none of the present oracles of hope is attributed to him. The second stage was an exilic editing of the book; its traces are to be found in 1.1, 5bc, 13bc, 2.3-5 and perhaps 10a, and 3.4. The addition of 'at that time' and the reference to 'the Spirit of Yahweh' in 3.8 also reflect an exilic point of view. In 6.14 the intrusive addition of 'and what you sow I will give to the sword' relates the judgment to defeat at the hands of the Babylonian armies, and the same exilic editorial hand is seen in the reference to the works of Omri and Ahab in v. 16. 6.1-8 and 7.1-6 are shown to be exilic by their parallels with Deuteronomy and Jeremiah respectively. Thus the exilic editor of the book interpreted the exile as judgment on the sin of the whole community and as a sign of the validity of the prophetic word. His view of the nature of the people's sin is close to that of the Deuteronomists and to Jeremiah and Ezekiel, who defined it chiefly in terms of religious apostasy and the 'prostitution' of religious syncretism. The third stage after the exile saw the definitive structuring of the book with the addition of the oracles of chs. 4–5, the final section of ch. 7, the glosses in 7.4b, 11-13 and the last line of v. 17. This gave a 'binary' structure to the book; oracles of judgment in chs. 1–3, hope of salvation in 4–5, judgment in 6.1–7.6 and hope in 7.7-20. This editor entertained a future eschatological hope in which he attempted to synthesize different Messianic ideas. He projected Micah's threats of judgment against Jerusalem on to a universal screen. The judgment had begun with the Babylonian exile. The return is imminent; but still to come are the assault of the nations against Jerusalem, the siege of the city and the humiliation of its ruler. However, all this will result in the final deliverance of Yahweh and the rule of a new David. Emphasis on the temple and on Jerusalem suggest that this editing comes from the priest-scribes of the post-exilic city; perhaps that is why it shows such close parallels to the Book of Haggai and to the work of the Chronicler. A final stage saw the removal of 2.12f. from its original place between 4.7 and 8 to its present position, so disturbing the binary pattern of the third editor. At this point there was some 're-reading' of earlier material in the light of the Samaritan schism (e.g. 1.5c; 6.16c) and this stage is therefore probably to be dated to the fourth century BCE.

The methods of form and redaction criticism may be said to have advanced beyond those of a criticism which concerned itself mainly with literary and historical matters. They have the great advantage of asking positive questions about the additions to the book; and they remind us that we are dealing with a living process by directing our attention to the purposes and methods of the various circles in which the material was handed down, re-interpreted and 're-read' in new situations. They force us to take the final form of the book seriously. Further, the considerable amount of agreement between the findings of our sample of scholars suggests that some such process must, in fact, have taken place. Yet, for all these gains, it has to be asked whether this type of criticism has not run into the same kind of dead-end as did literary criticism. Despite all the agreements between them, the substantial differences and variations in the picture each commentator

paints of the process show that here too the tools are far from
precise. A considerable subjective element remains. One
recent commentator on the book of Micah, D.R. Hillers (1984),
has been forthright about these limitations of the method:

> Redaction criticism of Micah fails to carry a satisfactory degree
> of conviction... We have only one form of the book, and nothing
> like direct evidence for the variety of text-forms the theory calls
> for... It would seem that a redaction criticism is hypothetical at
> too many points to be interesting (p. 3).

He goes on to accuse the exponents of the method of giving too
little attention to two factors, those of 'loss' and 'chance'.

> By loss I mean the accidental or deliberate omission of materials
> in the process of transmission (p. 4).

Redactors, he argues, may force a text to give the meaning
they want by means of excision; and of such activity, naturally,
we know nothing. He holds, furthermore, that the method

> underestimates the place that chance, the irrational, the unpre-
> dictable, may have in the forming of a text (*ibid.*).

The same objections can be levelled against attempts to find
a sophisticated literary plan or 'coherence' in the text as it now
stands, a method whose most notable exponent up to now has
been Hagstrom (1988). It is not that Hagstrom can in any way
be called a 'redaction critic'. He waves only a lofty and somewhat disdainful hand in passing at the problems of uncovering
the processes by which the text may have achieved its present
form. Yet his conviction that that final form reveals a complex,
carefully worked-out literary structure in which each part
has its significant and systematic place is open to exactly the
charges that Hillers makes against the methods of redaction
critics. Of course, the final form is not entirely incoherent.
Someone has given the material the shape and structure it has
in the form in which we now read it. Yet many tensions
remain in the text. The literary and redaction critics have not
been completely misled. The processes of growth and development must often have been haphazard and 'chancy'. On the
whole it is best to be cautious about claims to have discerned an
intricate pattern which has escaped everyone over many
centuries until one particular scholar wrote his thesis on the

book. Finding literary patterns is a subjective exercise and, as we have seen, different scholars can find different patterns and shapes in the material. This has been well expressed by Jeppesen (1987), who described the methods of the collectors and editors as 'users' of Micah's oracles who have used their scissors to cut from the Micah tradition what they needed for their situation, and who sometimes sewed the oracles together in a new pattern.

While, then, all methods of study of the text are valuable and offer real insights, the fact is that none of them, used singly or taken together, can offer us certainty. The element of the subjective must always remain; and while we may feel reasonably confident of what has happened in general, a degree of uncertainty about exactly how it has happened seems unavoidable. Have we run into the buffers of a terminus beyond which we cannot go? Hillers's own approach, despite his reservations about redaction criticism, is to assert the 'revitalization' of the text in new situations and among later generations; but this idea is not so different from much of what we have been considering. In our final section we turn to a form of this 'revitalization' which may offer a more satisfactory, if less ambitious, way forward.

Further Reading

G. Brin, 'Micah 2.12-13: A Textual and Ideological Study', *ZAW* 101 (1989), pp. 118-24.

H. Gunkel, 'The Close of Micah: A Prophetical Liturgy. A Study in Literary History', *in What Remains of the Old Testament?*, London, 1928, pp. 115-49.

D.G. Hagstrom, *The Coherence of the Book of Micah*, 1988.

B. Reicke, 'Liturgical Tradition in Micah 7', *HTR* 60 (1967), pp. 349-67.

J.M.P. Smith, *Micah, Zephaniah and Nahum*, ICC, 1911.

B.K. Waltke, *Obadiah, Jonah and Micah*, TOTC, 1988.

A.S. van der Woude, 'Three Classical Prophets', *in Israel's Prophetic Tradition*, ed. R.J. Coggins and others, Cambridge, 1982, pp. 32-57.

Works in foreign languages

K. Jeppesen, *Graeder ikke saa saare: Studier i Mikabogens sigte I-II*, Aarhus, 1987.

J. Jeremias, 'Die Deutung der Gerichtsworte Michas in der Exilzeit', *ZAW* 83 (1971), pp. 330-54.

T. Lescow (see Chapter 2, Futher Reading)

B. Renaud, *Structure et attaches littéraires de Michée iv–v*, Paris, 1964.

B. Renaud, *La formation du livre de Michée*, Paris, 1977.

T.H. Robinson, *Hosea bis Micha*, HAT 14/1, 1964[3].

W. Rudolph, *Micha–Nahum–Habakuk–Zephanja*, KAT, 1975.

I. Willi-Plein, *Verformen der Schriftexegese innerhalb des Alten Testaments*, 1971.

A.S. van der Woude, *Micha,* De prediking van het Oude Testament, Nijkerk, 2nd edn, 1977.

6

THE POST-EXILIC MESSAGE OF THE BOOK

ONE THING WHICH SEEMS to be beyond dispute is that, in its present form, the book of Micah is a post-exilic work. There is no doubt that it enshrines words of the historical Micah from the eighth century BCE. But equally, there can be no doubt that there have been additions to those words from different hands and from different times in the course of its transmission. For this reason it is extremely hazardous to attempt to reconstruct 'the message of Micah'. Some hints of what may have been the basic core of the message of the historical Micah have been given in Chapter 3, 'Micah the Man'. Jeppesen has rightly said, however, that it is very difficult to reconstruct the exact words of the original prophet (1987). What we can do here is to attempt to detect some of the interests and concerns of those who have made the additions, and guess a little at the different historical circumstances in which they may have been active. We can see some traces of editorial 'shaping' in the way the material is ordered. But all these things we see dimly; and the great variety of opinions about all of them shows the subjective element in our attempts and the limited conclusions to which we can hope to come.

Perhaps, therefore, it is best to read the book as a post-exilic work and ask how all these different elements have been taken up and used to address the people of Israel living in such very different circumstances from those in which Micah lived and worked. In this attempt also we have to build on the work of all those who have used every kind of method before us, and, just as much as they, we have to make subjective judgments about the material. But our claims are at least a little more limited. Rather than believing we can read the book 'diachronically', tracing the various stages by which it has been adapted across the years, we read it 'synchronically', accepting its final form and asking how that was used to address the situation after the exile. Jeppesen, whose work we have cited as typical of those who take this approach, believed that those who shaped the Micah material worked *during* the exile. They took actual pieces of cloth from Micah's own words but stitched them together to make a garment which would fit the needs of those in exile in Babylon. While there is no doubt an exilic element in the present book, the argument which will be advanced here is that parallels with much of the post-exilic literature suggest that, in the form in which we now have it, it was used also to address those who lived in Judah after 539 BCE (the date of the supposed 'decree' of Cyrus authorizing the exiles to return). We turn now, therefore, to a comparison of the main elements in the book of Micah with themes which occur in literature that we can safely date as 'post-exilic'.

(i) *The Oracles of Judgment*

We know that, after the exile, the warnings of the earlier prophets were held out as salutary lessons for later generations. The Chronicler records Hezekiah's appeal to the schismatic people of the old northern kingdom to return to God by coming to join the celebration of the Passover at the one, true sanctuary:

> Do not now be stiff-necked as your fathers were, but yield yourselves to the LORD, and come to his sanctuary... (2 Chron. 30.8).

Similar appeals elsewhere are linked directly to the calls of the prophets:

> Believe in the LORD your God, and you will be established; believe his prophets and you will succeed (2 Chron. 20.20).

Zechariah is recorded as uttering words remarkably similar to those of Hezekiah:

> Be not like your fathers, to whom the former prophets cried out, 'Thus says the LORD of hosts, Return from your evil ways and

from your evil deeds'. But they did not hear or heed me, says the
LORD (Zech. 1.4).

We may assume that Micah's words were preserved because
they were seen as one example of this witness to the fathers,
an assumption given extra weight by his appearance as just
such a prophet in Jer. 26.18f.:

> Micah of Moresheth prophesied in the days of Hezekiah king of
> Judah, and said to all the people of Judah: 'Thus says the LORD
> of hosts,
>> Zion shall be plowed as a field;
>>> Jerusalem shall become a heap of ruins,
>>> and the mountain of the house a wooded height'. Did
> Hezekiah king of Judah put him to death?
> Did he not fear the LORD, and did not the LORD repent of the evil
> which he had pronounced against them?

In Mic. 1.2-9 the prophet's cry against Samaria looks as
though it has been enlarged in scope by the addition of v. 2
which extends the address of the original word to the 'peoples'
and the 'earth', thus universalizing it. Verse 7 shows that
Samaria was attacked for its idolatry and the 'prostitution' of
its religious syncretism in a way very reminiscent of Hosea
(e.g. Hos. 3.12), of the Deuteronomists (e.g. 2 Kgs 17.7-18) and
of Jeremiah (e.g. Jer. 3.1-5). But these sins of Samaria characterized Judah as well, as is brought out by v. 5b, where

> What is the sin of Jacob?
> Is it not Samaria?

has been augmented by:

> What is the sin of the house of Judah?
> Is it not Jerusalem?

Thus 'all peoples', and, especially 'the house of Judah', have
been shown to be guilty of the same sins. We must be careful
before, with some scholars, we see later 'anti-Samaritan'
polemic here. The Samaritan religious community with its
temple on Mt Gerizim was a late development (see Coggins,
1975). Nevertheless there is no doubt that the Chronicler
believed that the northern kingdom had apostatized in seced-
ing from the Davidic dynasty and the Jerusalem temple. This
is well illustrated by the speech of Abijah appealing to the peo-

ple of the north to return (2 Chron. 13.4-12). Any kind of
alliance with the north was, to him, a sin for Judah. So Jeho-
shaphat is denounced by Eliezer for attempting a mercantile
venture with Ahaziah, a king of Israel, a venture which God
frustrated in judgment (2 Chron. 20.35-37). This is the kind of
outlook which would have found a warning for the present
time in Micah's threats against Samaria and would have felt
it wholly appropriate to add the question about Judah in 1.5b.
The prophet's lament in response to the arrival of the threat at
the gates of Jerusalem (1.9) underlines the same message; and
the description of the advance of an enemy brought by Yahweh in judgment, in which delight in word-play takes priority
over the description of any particular historical campaign,
would serve to highlight the general threat of divine judgment
at any period of the people's history when they were tempted
to indulge again in the 'northern-like' sin of religious apostasy.

Similarly the warning against the covetous and oppressive
ways of the rich and powerful (2.1-5; 3.1-4) can clearly be seen
as warnings for all times. The indignation of Nehemiah
against similar action by some of the community of his day
(Neh. 5.1-13) shows that the time of Micah had no monopoly
on such social and economic ills and injustices. Further, the
almost catechetical surveys of the ethical teaching of the earlier prophets found in Zechariah (7.8-14; 8.14-17), which
stress the enormity of the same practices ('...do not oppress
the widow, the fatherless, the sojourner or the poor...'), reit-
erate that it was failure to listen to such teaching which had
led to the loss of the land. All these show how pre-exilic
prophetical teaching was re-contextualized after the exile.
There is a close similarity between the predictions of disaster
on society in Mic. 3.5-12 and the retrospective glance at the
historical consequences of that disaster in Zech. 7.11-14 and
8.14, enough to show the relevance of such words of Micah to
the post-exilic situation. Even though they were then back in
the land the people were still not really masters of it, and were
still, therefore, to some extent under the judgment of God
(Ezra 9.6-15; Neh. 9.16-37). We are reminded how, in Trito-
Isaiah (Isa. 56–66) the suffering of which Second Isaiah (Isa.
40–55) speaks in describing the actual privations of the exile
in Babylon have become a more metaphorical description of

the continuing sufferings and privations experienced by the restored community in Palestine after the exile (e.g. Isa. 61.1-4, where the lamentations of the exiles have been replaced by the cries of 'those who mourn in Zion', v. 3).

The divine controversy (Heb. *rîb*, 'legal controversy') passage of 6.1-5, in which God brings a legal action against his people, calling on the mountains to act as witnesses, is a familiar pre-exilic prophetical device with parallels in Hos. 2.14-17; 4.1-10; Isa. 1.2f.; 3.13-15; cf. Ps. 50 (see Nielsen, 1978). The appeal to Yahweh's mercy at the time of the Exodus from Egypt and of other formative events in the nation's history is familiar from the Deuteronomistic literature and many of the Psalms. This does not mean that Micah cannot have expressed himself in this way, for there can be little doubt that the Deuteronomists were themselves influenced by the teaching of the eighth-century prophets. We have to be on our guard against excising every alleged 'Deuteronomism' from these prophets as evidence of later gloss. The response of the people (vv. 6f.), questioning how they may return, leads to the presentation of a prophetic 'Torah', teaching the ethical requirements of Yahweh's law. The whole passage thus forms something of a 'prophetic liturgy'. (This is the name given by form critics to passages in the prophetical writings in which the prophet seems to offer a 'liturgy' of words of prayer through which they might come to Yahweh, and then of answering words of God which they would hear if they did so. Hos. 14.1-7 is a good example of this: there v. 1 consists of a call to Israel to turn to God, 2f. gives them words by which to express their repentance, and vv. 4-7 provides Yahweh's answer to such a prayer.) Here in Micah the form is slightly different. It opens with a charge of Yahweh against the people (vv. 1f.), his appeal to them to return (vv. 3-5), the people's question as to how they may do this (vv. 6f.) and the oracular, divine answer (v. 8). There seems to be no compelling reason why the passage should not have come from Micah, or at least have been based on his words, with its parallels in other pre-exilic prophetic literature and, especially, its sharing with them concern for moral obedience rather than merely excessive cultic zeal. Nevertheless, 'oracular' guidance was clearly sought again in the post-exilic temple (e.g. Hag. 2.10-14; Zech.

7.2-4, 18f.); and, again, the Micah oracle reads remarkably like the summaries of the teaching of the prophets already alluded to in Zech. 7.9f. and 8.16f. Compare

> Render true judgments (lit. judge true *mišpāṭ*), show kindness (*ḥesed*) and mercy... (Zech. 7.9).

with

> and what does the LORD require of you
> but to do justice (*mišpāṭ*) and to love kindness (*ḥesed*)...? (Mic. 6.8).

We need not suppose specific and direct dependence of any kind between the two passages, but such general similarities show how well the Micah passage would lend itself to a post-exilic reading of the book.

In the same way, the denunciation of social sins in 6.9-12 could have fitted the pre-exilic time of Micah, for it echoes charges made in Amos and Isaiah. Yet the announcement of judgment (vv. 13-15) is reminiscent of Haggai's words in Hag. 1.6 and 2.17. Certainly the reference to 'the sword' in v. 14d, interrupting the rhythm of the lines, appears to extend the judgment to include the defeat which led to the exile, while the reference in v. 16 to the 'statutes of Omri' and the 'works of the house of Ahab' also expresses rejection of 'northern-like' religious syncretism and apostasy. A very similar vocabulary to that of v. 16 is found in Jeremiah (19.8; 25.9, 18; 29.18; 51.37), all but the last occurring in the 'Deuteronomistic' sections of the book. Again, therefore, it looks as though a specific warning of Micah to the Judah of his day has been given a wider prophetic reference, and that its scope has been extended to challenge a later generation, which knew the disaster of the exiles to be on its guard. Unlike the fathers, they must 'hear the words of the former prophets'.

Even the account of Micah's dispute with the 'pseudo-prophets' (2.6-11) would have recalled to later generations the conflict between 'true' and 'false' prophecy which is so prominent a theme in Deuteronomy and in the Deuteronomic Book of Jeremiah. Its effect would have been to assure the hearers of the authenticity of Micah's preaching which was now being pressed upon them.

(ii) *The Promises of Salvation*
It can be no coincidence that, in the present structure of the
book, the prediction of total destruction of Jerusalem and its
society (3.9-12) is followed immediately by a promise that this
judgment will be reversed in every particular. The city which
was to be laid low as a heap of ruins will be 'raised up above the
hills' (4.1). The place where the priests 'taught for hire' (3.11)
will become the place to which the nations come 'that he may
teach us his ways' (4.2). The city whose rulers 'abhorred justice' (Heb. *mišpāṭ*) will be the place where God will 'judge'
(Heb. *šāpaṭ*—the verb from which the noun 'justice' derives)
all nations (4.3). The place where the leaders claimed in
unfounded confidence, 'Is not the LORD in the midst of us?'
(3.11; cf. Ps. 46.7, 11), in a shallow perversion of the 'Zion theology' which saw the city as God's chosen dwelling place (e.g.
Ps. 132.13-18) will be the goal of the nations in their pilgrimage, now in the justified confidence that they will encounter
him in 'the house of the God of Jacob' (4.2). God's reign as universal king, settling the disputes of all nations as they
acknowledge his sovereignty, will result in peace and plenty,
where previously the poor were flayed and devoured by the
wealthy and powerful (3.1-3). When in that blood-stained city
the leaders called on Yahweh he would not answer them (3.4);
but in the future people will seek him there and find him (4.2).
Thus the post-exilic community is reminded of the grace of
God which will revoke the just punishment for former sins
and inaugurate the new era of the divine kingdom of justice
and peace. This is exactly the message of a prophet like Second
Isaiah who announces God's intention to save his people, now
that they have suffered fully for all their sins (e.g. Isa. 40.1f., 9-
11; 43.25-28; 52.1f.; etc.).

It is therefore idle to ask whether 4.1-4 (= Isa. 2.2-4) is
'originally' by either Isaiah or Micah. It is by neither; but its
presence in both books shows how the prophetic collections
were treated in order to make them relevant to later generations.

To this new kingdom the exiles will be brought back according to an oracle (4.6f.) which may have rested on a promise of
Micah to the dispossessed poor after their rulers were punished, but has now been transformed into an oracle assuring

those who have been 'driven away' into exile and 'cast off' that
they will be 'brought back' by Yahweh, again to become a
'strong nation' under his rule in the new 'kingdom of God'
centred on Zion.

Yet it is instructive to see how, between two such oracles of
hope, an admonitory note has been inserted in v. 5.

> For all the peoples walk
> each in the name of its god,
> but we will walk in the name of the LORD our God
> for ever and ever.

Apparently, this post-exilic glossator does not yet see this universal rule of God, nor does he see evidence of all nations coming to acknowledge Yahweh as king. But let his people walk
faithfully in obedience to him meanwhile, to prove worthy of
hope which is before them. Such hortatory 'preaching' is
clearly a mark of the post-exilic period. We see it in the second
half of Zech. 6.15, summing up all the great hopes of the
visions of the prophet:

> And this shall come to pass, if you will diligently obey the voice
> of the LORD your God.

It can also be found in Mal. 4.4 [3.22], which follows the
promises of the prophet of the coming judgment of God when
the wicked will be judged but the righteous set free with a
warning to 'Remember the law of my servant Moses...' It is
heard in the ethical summaries of the teaching of the former
prophets in Zech. 7–8 and in the general exhortation of Zech.
1.1-6. It is a feature, as we have seen, of many of the speeches
in the books of Chronicles. So, after the exile, the faith of the
people was stimulated by a renewal of the prophetic promises
of old, but with a pastoral call to the community to keep the
faith during the present time of waiting (see Mason, 1990).

It looks as though a promise, similar to those found in 4.1-4,
6-8, has been constructed out of an original threat of the exact
opposite in 2.13, and it is small wonder that a number of commentators have believed that 2.12f. belonged originally in
ch. 4. The threat of siege and its disastrous end in 2.13 has been
transformed by the addition of v. 12 into an oracle of hope of

salvation when God gathers his people, like the good shepherd
of Ezekiel 34. This is a 'reversal of judgment' theme indeed.

In some ways even the oracles of hope reflect a background
of a present time of distress and judgment. This is true of 2.12f.
and of a passage such as 4.6-8. In this way also they may be
said to resemble Second Isaiah, whose oracles address themselves to the laments of a people suffering present tribulation
(see J. Jeremias). So the need of the people of the eighth century, expressed once by Micah, also offers a point of re-application when, in the post-exilic period, the people still await the
promised glorious future in a time yet racked by tension and
frustration (cf. the encouragement and exhortations of Trito-
Isaiah). This gives 'contemporaneity' to such a passage as 4.9-
11 which speaks of the 'now' of the time when Jerusalem is
besieged and facing exile. But this historic occasion furnishes a
figure for the 'assault of the nations' theme that is based on
Psalm passages such as those in Ps. 48.4-8 and in Isa. 29.1-8
but which, in later prophetic passages, becomes the birthpangs
of the new age of God's final deliverance (Zech. 12.1-5; 14.1-5;
cf. v. 9; and cf. Renaud's analysis of the 'post-exilic' stage of the
editing of the book). Micah's preaching has thus provided a
basis for a more general eschatological hope in this 'reversal of
judgment' theme which can be related to present unfulfilled
hopes and at the same time offer the basis for a re-affirmation
of the certainty of the fulfilment of those hopes in the future.

Not only is the situation in Zion to be completely reversed,
but its erstwhile false leaders are to be replaced (5.2-4 [1-3]) by
a leader who will truly 'shepherd' and 'feed' the flock, offering
it lasting security. It is interesting that the term 'king' (Heb.
melek) is not used, just as it is avoided in Ezek. 40–48.
Nevertheless the 'shepherding' motif links the role of this
'ruler' in Israel with that of the kings, since 'shepherd' was a
widespread descriptive title of kings in the ancient Near East,
while the reference to Bethlehem presumably associates the
Sheperd with the Davidic line. His appearance too, whatever
exact picture is being offered of a 'messianic' leader here, follows a time of travail and is again marked by a return from
exile. Such speculation about a true leadership is another
marked feature of the post-exilic literature, with Haggai's
hopes about Zerubbabel (2.20-23) and Zechariah's picture of a

joint rule of priest and governor (4.14), while the later chapters of Zechariah also speak of a coming 'king' (9.9f.). It is natural enough that these prophets, as well as the Chronicler
with his picture of David and Second Isaiah with his apparent
re-interpretation of the Davidic covenant (Isa. 55.3-5), should
reflect what must have been a major concern of the post-exilic
community bereft of the dynasty whose unbroken rule had
been earlier promised (2 Sam. 7.12-17).

5.10-15 [9-14] looks as though it might originally have been
a threat to the Judah of Micah's day directed against Israel's
religious syncretism and trust in the strength of human
armies. Now, however, in its present context, it has become a
promise of the cleansing of the community by the grace of God
in preparation for the new age, an age which will be marked
by the defeat of those nations who had threatened Israel and
whose influence had also led them away from Yahweh (5-9 [4-
7]; cf. Zech. 1.14-16, 18-20; 2.8-12 [12-16]). The realization of
the need for the community to be cleansed from its sins and
from the contamination of the nations is yet another post-
exilic prophetic note, particularly found in Zech. 3.1-5 in the
version of the cleansing of the priest as representative of the
whole people (cf. Zech. 5.1-11).

The post-exilic form of the book, therefore, insists that the
last word will be, not with the sin of the nation and with judgment, but with the grace and redeeming power of God. The
judgments of which Micah warned are to be exactly reversed,
the community cleansed and the people given a share in Yahweh's triumphant universal rule in which all of his, and their,
enemies will be overcome. The terms in which all this is
announced are clearly paralleled in the exilic and post-exilic
prophets, in Second Isaiah, Ezekiel, Haggai, Zechariah (1–8)
and also in the later chapters (9–14) of the book of Zechariah.
Yet all this is combined with the renewal and extension of the
warnings of the original prophet which, together with isolated
admonitory notes, remind the people that they must show
themselves worthy of this destiny by their obedience to God's
words through the prophets in a way that their fathers sign-
ally failed to do.

(iii) *The Concluding Liturgy*

Chapter 7, in the striking form of a prophetic liturgy, brings home the basic theology of the book. Verses 1-6 contain a poetic lament in which the prophet speaks on behalf of the whole community, bewailing the present state of evil and distress, with its hunger and its deep divisions in society, in terms reminiscent of Haggai (1.6-11; 2.15-17) and Ezekiel (22.7). In vv. 7-10 the prophet submits to God's judgment and is assured of his deliverance. This results in a divine oracle announcing the rebuilding of the city, the return of the exiles and the overthrow of the oppressor nations (vv. 11-13, all themes which occur in Second Isaiah as well as in the prophets of the restoration). A renewed prayer of trust calling on Yahweh to act as their true king ('Shepherd thy people with thy staff', vv. 14f.), leads on to another oracle proclaiming the defeat of the nations (vv. 16f.) A triumphant affirmation of faith in the mercy and goodness of God brings assurance of his salvation in the future (vv. 18-20). Parallels to other such prophetic liturgies (e.g. Hos. 14.1-7), to some of the Psalms and to Lamentations show that here the theological statements of the book and general post-exilic prophetic themes have passed over into the language of worship.

The book of Micah, then, shows how the words of a pre-exilic prophet could become the text for a proclamation of the certainty of God's salvation for the people who had suffered, and in many ways were still suffering, the judgments of which the prophet had spoken. The prophet's words furnished the material for preaching and worship in the post-exilic period. The post-exilic book of Micah is thus a call for faith in and obedience to a God whose purpose is to have mercy and to deliver his people.

Further Reading

R.J. Coggins, *Samaritans and Jews*, Oxford, 1975.

K. Nielsen, *Yahweh as Prosecutor and Judge*, Sheffield, 1978.

R.A. Mason, *Preaching the Tradition: Homily and Hermeneutic after the Exile*, Cambridge, 1990.

NAHUM

Select List of Commentaries

E. Achtemeier, *Nahum–Malachi*, Interpretation, Atlanta, 1986. More exegetical and devotional than scholarly. Useful for preachers.

D.W. Baker, *Nahum, Habbakkuk, Zephaniah*, TOTC, London, 1988. Extremely conservative to the point where preconceived ideas appear to determine conclusions.

R.J. Coggins, *Israel among the Nations: A Commentary on the Books of Nahum and Obadiah*, ITC, Grand Rapids and Edinburgh, 1985. The best of recent commentaries, emphasizing the function and cultic setting of such prophecy.

J.H. Eaton, *Obadiah, Nahum, Habakkuk, Zephaniah*, TBC, London, 1961. An early work already prefiguring the author's later emphases on the place of prophecy in cultic drama.

J.P. Hyatt, 'Nahum', *Peake's Commentary on the Bible* (revised edn), London, 1962, pp. 635-36. In very short space the author surveys the main critical issues and tries to 'rescue' Nahum from current adverse judgment.

J.M.P. Smith, *A Critical and Exegetical Commentary on Nahum*, ICC, Edinburgh, 1911. Still useful in its encyclopaedic survey of research up to that time and in its treatment of the Hebrew text, with full attention to issues which still engage critical attention.

R.L. Smith, *Micah–Malachi*, Word Biblical Commentary, Waco, 1984. To the writer's own shrewd, fairly conservative judgments is added a very useful survey of much recent scholarly discussion.

C.L. Taylor, Jr, 'The Book of Nahum', *IB*, VI, 1956, pp. 953-69. The writer does not have a great deal of sympathy with Nahum but offers careful examination of the text and its difficulties.

J.D.W. Watts, *The Books of Joel, Obadiah, Jonah, Nahum, Habakkuk and Zephaniah*, CBC, Cambridge, 1975. The readership aimed at in this series was so wide and the space so severely rationed that they serve best as an introduction to study of any particular biblical book.

Commentaries in foreign languages

B. Renaud, *Michée, Sophonie, Nahum*, Paris, 1987.

R. Vuilleumier and C.A. Keller, *Michée, Nahoum, Habacuc, Sophonie*, Commentaire de Ancien Testament, Neuchâtel, 1971.

K. Elliger, *Die Propheten Nahum, Habakuk, Zephanja, Haggai, Sacharja, Maleachi*, ATD 25, 1964.

G. Horst, *Die zwölf kleinen Propheten*, HAT, 1971.

1

NAHUM
AMONG THE
PROPHETS

A N ISRAELITE KING, AHAB, once said of a prophet (Mica-iah), 'I hate him, for he never prophesies good concerning me, but evil' (1 Kgs 22.8). Had they lived in the same century (in fact two hundred years divided them) he might have thought more highly of Nahum as a prophet. In the three chapters of Nahum there is not a hint of criticism of the Judah of the seventh century BCE, nor a whisper of threat of judgment against the people for their sins (at least in the book as it stands now). On the contrary, all its anger is reserved for Israel's enemies—the great power of Assyria is the only one mentioned by name—and it declares God's judgment against those enemies while summoning the people of God to joyful celebration of salvation (1.15 [2.1]). This is very different from Micah and most of the other eighth- and seventh-century prophets.

Where Ahab might have approved of Nahum, however, many modern commentators have not. J.M.P. Smith speaks for many when he says that, in place of the preoccupation of other prophets with the sins of Israel, 'there appears a certain fiery form of indignation against Judah's ancient foe, which exhibits a degree of animosity for which the great ethical prophets furnish no parallel' (1911, p. 280). Indeed, with Nahum, he believes, 'a representative of the old, narrow and shallow prophetism finds its place in the Canon of Scripture' (p. 281). Nor has Smith lacked his more recent supporters. Taylor finds in Nahum 'a reversion to that nationalistic, chauvinistic type of prophecy represented by the four hundred with whom Micaiah ben Imlah contended (1 Kgs 22), and from which Amos dissociated himself' (1956, p. 953).

Adjectives like 'non-ethical', 'complacent', and even 'false' have all been used of Nahum, and these are not the most likely to encourage us to set out on the study of the book. Yet some more recent studies have counselled greater caution before dismissing him too brusquely. They have reminded us that most of the major prophetic collections have sections of oracles against foreign nations not very dissimilar from those found here. Second Isaiah (the exilic prophet of Isa. 40–55) also predicts defeat and judgment for the enemy (Babylon) and salvation for Israel, while the overthrow of God's (and so his people's) enemies and the deliverance of his people are themes prominent in much of the so-called 'apocalyptic' literature of the Old Testament. If we start by excising Nahum from our theologically and ethically approved canon of scripture we may find a great deal more work for our editorial scissors before we have finished.

Nahum deserves our attention, then; but if we examine the book with too narrow a lens we may distort it. We shall not read it properly unless we see it as part of 'The Book of the Twelve' (the name given in the Hebrew canon to what are often described as 'The Minor Prophets'), the 'Prophets' as a whole, and, indeed, the entire canon. Here, if ever, there is a case, not only for the textual analysis and dissection of the more traditional approaches, but for what is often called today a 'canonical' reading (see Childs, 1979). However, it is a peculiarity of Childs's approach to this issue that he considers the canonical form and its significance for interpretation only *within* each individual book. He does not go on to ask what its final placing in the canon as a whole has done for the way we are meant to read it. We must place the book in a larger context before we can assess it in proper terms. Just what this may mean for the way we read and understand Nahum will become clear as our discussion progresses and, especially, in Chapter 6.

2

NAHUM
AND HIS
TIMES

NOTHING IS KNOWN TO US about the man Nahum. The superscription says that he came from Elkosh, but the location of his town is as much a matter of guesswork as the man himself. His name means 'comfort'. This fits well with the message of the book and since, as we shall see, parallels have been found between this book and Second Isaiah, it is interesting that Second Isaiah opens with the twice repeated use of the verb from which Nahum's name comes, 'naḥᵃmû, naḥᵃmû (comfort, comfort), my people, says your God'. Coggins (1985, p. 6) says that the lack of any biographical knowledge about the prophet may well be an advantage since in recent times attention has moved away from a 'psychological' study of the prophets as individuals. He might have added that it has also moved away from attempts to 'date' oracles by supposed references to particular historical events allegedly to be found in them. Instead, it has concentrated more on the function of prophecy and its place in the life and worship of the confessional community from which it came and which preserved it. His own insistence that the cult (the formal worship of the sanctuaries, in this case the Jerusalem temple) was the 'home' of much of Nahum's prophecy has, as we shall see, much to commend it.

There are, as it happens, two specific historical events mentioned in the book. The first (in chronological order) is the sack of the Egyptian city of Thebes, called Nō'-'āmôn in 3.8, by Esarhaddon, king of Assyria. He brought it under Assyrian control in 670 BCE but finally captured it in 661 BCE. The other is the fall of Nineveh in 612 BCE to Cyaxares the Mede, in alliance with the Babylonians after a siege of three months. We might suppose from this that we are able to pinpoint Nahum somewhere in the period between 661 and 612, as is done by many commentators. Yet there are at least two difficulties in using 'historical' references to date prophetic books. The first is that it is by no means clear when a prophet is referring to a past event and when he is predicting something yet to happen in the future. That is because of the rhetorical device known to Hebraists as 'the prophetic perfect'. This partly explains why commentators have been divided in their opinions as to whether Nahum is predicting the fall of Nineveh, or is describing something which has already taken place.

The other problem with 'historical' references in the prophetic books is that they may have had at the time the original prophet used them, or have acquired later among those who passed on his words, a symbolic meaning. An example of this occurs in the book of Revelation which talks about Babylon: 'Fallen, fallen is Babylon the great' (14.8). Of course, the historical city of Babylon had fallen centuries before. It is the fall of Rome which is being announced (in a 'prophetic perfect'). 'Babylon' has become a symbol of the oppressive powers of this world of which, for the Christian church, Rome was all too typical a later example. It is quite possible that the book of Nahum uses 'Nineveh' in such a way and, if that were so, we could no more 'date' it by the fall of the historical city of Nineveh than we could date the author of 'Revelation' by the fall of the historical city of Babylon. Alternatively, actual words of an historical seventh-century Nahum may have come to be vested with a symbolic meaning in the course of time, and may have this meaning in the book in its present form. This has been powerfully argued by, among others, Schulz (1973).

However, it seems safe to assume that there was a prophet Nahum somewhere behind the present book, and that he lived in the time of Assyrian domination over Judah and over much of the ancient Near East, probably towards the time of the decline and fall of that empire. We saw how Micah lived in the shadow cast by the rise of Assyrian power. Manasseh, king of Judah (687-642 BCE) was a vassal of Assyria throughout his reign. The great Assyrian king Ashurbanipal (668-627) was the king who sacked Thebes in 661 (Nah. 3.8). But by the end of his reign Assyria was already being menaced by the combined threat of the Medes and the Babylonians. Soon after Ashurbanipal's death these inflicted a defeat on the Assyrians just outside Babylon in 626. In 614 the capital city of Asshur fell to Cyaxares the Mede, and two years later Cyaxares and Nabopolassar of Babylon took Nineveh. So, if Micah may be said to have witnessed the dawn of the Assyrian empire, Nahum celebrated its sunset.

Further Reading

B.S. Childs, *Introduction to the Old Testament as Scripture*, London, 1979.

H. Schulz, *Das Buch Nahum*, BZAW 129, 1973.

J. Bright, *A History of Israel*, 3rd edn, pp. 310-16.

B. Oded, 'Judah and the Exile', in *Israelite and Judaean History*, ed. J.H. Hayes and J.M. Miller, 1977, especially pp. 466f.

3

THE CONTENTS
OF THE BOOK

A S WITH THE BOOK OF MICAH there is a wide variety in the
ways in which commentators divide the book of Nahum
into its various sections; the greatest differences are to be
found in their treatment of 1.2–2.2 (3). One possible division is
as follows:

(i)	1.1	Superscription.
(ii)	1.2-8	Acrostic poem announcing the theophany ('appear–ance', or 'coming') of Yahweh.
(iii)	1.9–2.2 [3]	Alternating threats of judgment against Yahweh's enemies and promises of deliverance to his people.
(iv)	2.3-12 [4-13]	Poem(s) describing the defeat of Yahweh's enemy identified in v. 8 with Nineveh.
(v)	2.13 [14]	Prose oracle threatening judgment.
(vi)	3.1-4	A 'woe' oracle describing the battle and lamenting the defeat of the 'city of blood'.
(vii)	3.5-19	An oracle of judgment addressed to Nineveh in the second person.

To divide the book into sections as we have done here is not to
argue that each of them has existed from the first as a complete unit in its present form. Abrupt changes of subject, of persons addressed, now in the plural, now the singular, now masculine, now feminine, changes of metre and of imagery, all
suggest that originally disparate material has been brought
together, whether by the prophet himself or others. Nowhere
is this more evident than in 1.9–2.2 [3], 2.10-12 [11-13] and
2.13 [14]; but it is true of each section to some extent. Often it is
far from clear just who is being addressed or spoken about.
The inference is that, rather than seeing the book as the com-

3. *The Contents of the Book*

position of one prophet at one time, we should think of it as an 'anthology' of prophetic and cultic material which has been shaped for a particular purpose. This also means that it is impossible always to be sure just where one section ends and another begins; and that is why a number of commentators have argued for more small sub-divisions in their conception of the plan of the book than has been suggested here. Some have also made various suggestions for re-arranging the text in order to get a more 'logical' order. While it is always possible that dislocation has taken place, recognition of the nature of the book as an 'anthology' should make us wary of expecting too ordered and logical a progression of thought and amending the text accordingly.

While it is impossible here to give a detailed commentary on the whole text of the book it is important, before we consider some of the critical questions it raises for interpretation and the various answers scholars have offered, to start from the biblical text itself, its main features and characteristics of style and form, its particular theological insights and the viewpoints which find expression in it. We therefore give a brief survey of each of the main sections outlined above.

1.1. *The Superscription*
There is a double heading at the start of the book. The Hebrew term translated 'An *oracle* concerning Nineveh' means literally 'a *burden*'; this became a technical term for a prophetic oracle. As such it occurs repeatedly in the section of oracles against foreign nations in the book of Isaiah (e.g. 13.1, 'the oracle concerning Babylon which Isaiah saw...'; 15.1 'an oracle concerning Moab'; etc.). This is interesting because, as we have already mentioned, some recent commentators have argued that Nahum is strikingly similar to the kind of material which comprises the oracles against the nations in the major prophetical books.

The second part of the superscription links the book firmly with prophecy by the use of the term 'vision'; but it is also important to note that this is the only place where any prophetical collection is referred to as a 'book'. This might indicate that Nahum was in written form from the first. 'Nahum is self-consciously a piece of literature' (R.L. Smith,

p. 71). More probably, however, it shows an advance towards
the stage at which the prophetic collections were committed to
writing, a stage represented later, in the second century BCE,
in Daniel: 'I, Daniel, perceived in the books...' (9.2). (The next
verse makes it clear that he was reading Jeremiah.) We know
very little of the process by which the prophetic collections
achieved their present written form, but this must have been
happening during the post-exilic period, since post-exilic literature contains an increasing number of quotations from the
prophetic books.

1.2-8 Acrostic Poem Announcing the Theophany of Yahweh
The first section of the book is an alphabetic acrostic: that is, a
poem in which the successive lines or short units begin with
letters following the order of the alphabet. It was Franz
Delitzsch who in his Psalms commentary (1859), speaking of
such an acrostic in Psalm 9, was the first to point to a similar
structure in Nah. 1.3-7. Today it is generally agreed that this
acrostic goes as far as the letter *kaph* in v. 8 and that the poem
ends there. The NEB is a notable exception to this; but it has
achieved a continuation of the acrostic down to v. 14 only by
drastic rearrangement of the text. The more usual view was
expressed by Elliger and de Vries (1966). In fact the letters
aleph to *kaph* represent exactly half the Hebrew alphabet,
eleven letters out of twenty-two. Renaud (1987, p. 276) points
out that *kaph* in v. 8 is the first letter of the Hebrew word
kālâh which means not only 'to make a full end' but a 'full
accomplishment' or 'achievement' and so marks a fitting climax to the announcement of Yahweh's appearance in judgment. An acrostic form may seem artificial to us, but N.K.
Gottwald (*Studies in the Book of Lamentations*, London, 1962,
pp. 23f.), writing of the same phenomenon in that book, says
that it represents a completeness of both judgment and peni-
tence or, as we might say, 'The A-Z of God's purposes'. Others
have seen a magical element in its use, but Coggins makes a
useful observation when he says that all the uses of the acrostic form 'appear to have been related to the Jerusalem cult'
(p. 19).
    The poem itself speaks of Yahweh entirely in the third per-
son. It uses vocabulary and imagery familiar from many

psalms which depict the theophany. It also echoes elements from Canaanite religious epics and has much in common with eschatological elements in other Old Testament prophecy. The Canaanite background is especially clear in v. 2 where the two epithets Ba'al and El, both names of Canaanite deities, are found, a fact noted by Cathcart (p. 40). Further, v. 3d recalls the description of Ba'al as 'The Rider of the Clouds' in the Canaanite religious epics. Indeed, J. Gray says of Nahum 1, 'In the depiction of God (in v. 3) it is possible to see a reference to Jahweh in the Sinai theophany, but it is more natural to see the imagery of the theophany of Ba'al, the Canaanite Storm God' (1961, pp. 16f.; cf. 1956, p. 280). However, such vocabulary was probably already subsumed into the Jerusalem liturgy, and it is this which is most naturally to be seen as the ground common both to Nahum 1 and to similar material in the psalms and the prophetic literature. Such a background would explain why there is no specific reference to Nineveh here.

1.9–2.2 [3] *Alternating Threats of Judgment and Promises of Deliverance*
This section is marked not only by the switches in mood between threats and promises, but also of the person and gender of speaker and of those addressed. There is third person reference to the divine speaker (vv. 9, 11; 2.2 [3]) but also the first person of divine speech (12, 13, 14); there are allusions to persons spoken about in the third person (vv. 10, 12, 13), while others are addressed directly in the second person (9, 11, 12b, 13, 14, 15b [2.1b]; 2.1 [2]). Even here there is a difference between a masculine 'you' and a feminine (masculine in 9a, 14a, 14b, 14d; feminine in 11a, 12b, 13a, 15b [2.1b], 2.1a [2a]). It is, therefore, far from clear exactly who is being addressed.

Where so much is obscure it would be rash to dogmatize. No doubt part of the confusion is due to the fact that the material is of composite origin. (We find equally sharp switches of mood and address in a similar kind of 'eschatological' collection in Zech. 9.11-17 and, indeed, in many other such places.) Again we notice that here, as in the psalm, no particular enemy is specified, but quite a number of general themes are expressed. The verb 'to plot' used of human rebellion against God appears in the Psalms (e.g. 35.4; 41.7 [8]). It is given an historical 'actualization' by Isaiah when speaking of the pride and arrogance of the king of Assyria who refuses to keep to his God-appointed bounds: 'But he does no so intend and his mind does not so *think*' (Isa. 10.7; the Hebrew verb is the same), 'Villainy' (v. 11) is, in Hebrew, the word 'Belial', which suggests that, whatever particular historical manifestation of it might have been in the mind of the prophet, it is but a symptom of a more general, 'demonic' expression of evil, of all that is opposed to God.

Many have noted that there is a close parallel between 1.15 [2.1] and Isa. 52.7. Nahum reads:

> Look, on the mountains
> the feet of the messenger
> proclaiming salvation (Heb. *šālôm*)

Isa. 52.7 reads:

> How beautiful on the mountains
> are the feet of the messenger
> proclaiming salvation (Heb. *šālôm*) [author's translations].

All these 'generalizing' tendencies in 1.9–2.2 [3] may suggest that we are dealing with 'traditional' prophetic material drawn perhaps from different sources, rather than with *ad hoc* composition by one prophet in one particular historical context. Perhaps, as Coggins suggests, all such material had its origin in the cult (pp. 33f.).

2.3-12 [4-13] *Poem(s) Describing the Defeat of God's Enemy (Nineveh)*

This section comprises a vivid, almost 'impressionistic' poem portraying the attack on Nineveh. Because of its impressionistic nature it is idle to expect a war correspondent's detailed and factual account of an actual battle. The interest is in onomatopoeia, alliteration, assonance and vivid imagery to reproduce the sights, the sounds, the fury, the confusion and the horror of a battle in process (see Chapter 4 below). That is undoubtedly why a number of details are obscure.

What is clear is that there is to be a reversal of judgment. The attackers will be attacked, the oppressors oppressed, the plunderer plundered (a familiar theme in later prophecy, e.g. Jer. 51.44; Ezek. 33.2-10; Zech. 1.18-21 [2.1-4]). The picture of the oppressor nations who have preyed like marauding lions on the weak and defenceless now being themselves defeated by Yahweh is also found in later prophecy (e.g. Jer. 51.38-40) and featured in Israel's worship (e.g. Ps. 58.6 [7]). The addition of the prose oracle in v. 13 [14] drives this lesson home. It has been placed where it is not only by this continuity of theme but by the editorial device of a 'catchword' link, in this case the word 'young lions'. It could have come straight from such a late collection of oracles as those found in Jer. 51 which are applied in a similar fashion to the downfall of a tyrant, in that case Babylon.

In all, the very general nature of the account of the attack and the mythical allusions and parallels to the vocabulary, imagery and themes of mainly later prophecy all seem to confirm the impression that an original account of an attack on Nineveh is here being portrayed as a final encounter between Yahweh and the forces of chaos, the powers of this world. A particular historical episode has been projected on to a cosmic screen. Renaud (1987, p. 297) has said, 'As we come to see it in its actual context the name (of Nineveh) carries an eschatological dimension, and the battle corresponds to the great conflict at the end of time. However, that is a matter of its (later) re-interpretation, for originally these verses announced the fall of the historical Nineveh.'

3.1-4 A 'Woe' Oracle
This oracle is introduced by the Hebrew word *hôy*, usually translated 'woe'. It represents the desolated cry of the mourner; and so the oracle becomes a funeral dirge. This too gives a vivid, breathless portrayal of an attack, seemingly with no time for verbs. A literal rendering of the Hebrew runs as follows:

> The crack of a whip
> and the vibrating wheel,
> the galloping horse
> and the jolting chariot...

The poet is again either (ironically) lamenting over the fall of
Nineveh as a past event, or is so sure of its coming that he acts
already, in anticipation, the part of the mourner. It is interesting to note that this is the second reference in this short book to
pagan religious practices as one major cause of the divine
judgment (cf. 1.14). This also is a feature of later, eschatological oracles (e.g. Isa. 65.1-7; Zech. 13.2-6; Mal. 3.5).

3.5-19 *An Oracle of Judgment Addressed to Nineveh*

In this section, which may again have been comprised a number of originally separate units, it is significant that for the
third time there is an allusion to religious paganism (cf. 1.14;
3.4) in terms in which a number of prophets had attacked
Israel. This impression is strengthened by the use of the
Hebrew *šiqquṣîm,* 'detestable things', RSV 'filth', a term used
by the editors of the books of Kings, the book of Deuteronomy
and prophets like Hosea, Jeremiah and Ezekiel as well as by
the exilic Priestly law code.

A further interesting point about this particular threatened
punishment emerges. Cathcart (1973) has claimed that this is
one of a number of threats which reflect treaty-curses. These
occur in many ancient Near Eastern political treaties; they
functioned as sanctions against whoever broke the treaty
terms. Other threats include the breaking of the staff (cf. Nah.
1.13), denying descendants to the king (1.14; 3.18), and the
breaking of weapons (2.13[14]), as well as being stripped like a
prostitute. Cathcart finds the greatest number of such parallels in the book of Jeremiah. Since Israel was so often threatened by the prophets with a judgment which fulfilled the
covenant curses of such passages as Deut. 26, this affords yet
another example of the tables being turned. Now these same
threats are to fall on Israel's enemy. The corollary, that God
will remember covenant mercy to Israel, is made explicit in
1.12f., 15 [2.1], 2.2 [3].

The difficulty of taking the description of Thebes in 3.8 literally (the sea was forty miles to the north of it!) has led many
to see here another mythological reference to the primeval
conflict between God and the waters of chaos, with Thebes
thus being treated as another symbol of human might, splen-
dour and pomp, opposed to God's rule. This is the view of Hal-

dar who sees 'the streams' as indicating the rivers of the
nether world (p. 139). Recent commentators who have agreed
with this view include Coggins, and R.L. Smith, who says, 'All
the references to the sea and waters in v. 8 seem to go beyond a
factual description of the city's position' (p. 88). In any event,
the irony of the enquiry addressed to Nineveh implies that it
deserves no better a fate.

In what follows, a succession of prophetic judgment themes
are sounded: the futility of human allies in the face of God's
judgment (vv. 9f.; cf. Isa. 31.1-4); the terrible fate of the most
helpless citizens, the babies and the children (cf. Ps. 137.9; Isa.
13.16); the dishonouring of the nobility (cf. Isa. 3.1-5; Amos 4.1-
3). Reeling under God's judgment as if drunk is another
prophetic theme (Jer. 25.15-17; Ezek. 23.32-34). In a series of
hammer-blows the reversal of all these themes as they are
turned from Israel towards Nineveh is driven home. The
repetition of the Hebrew word *gam* ('even') sounds the blows:
'Even she was carried away...'; 'even her little ones...' (v. 10);
and, in v. 11, 'Even you will be drunk. . .; even you will seek...'
The panic which reduces its soldiers to the alleged weakness of
women (v. 13) is yet another prophetic theme (cf. Isa. 19.16),
while the entrance of the enemy because the defensive bolts on
the gates have been burned down is found in Amos 1.4, 7, 10,
12, 14; 2.2, 5. For all the numbers the enemy could muster,
until their advancing army seemed like a plague of locusts
(v. 15), and for all the wealth its traders have brought its, all
will be swept away as a swarm of locusts is dispersed from its
shelter by the warmth of the sun (cf. the oracle against Tyre in
Ezek. 38).

The theme of the attack on the 'shepherds', the kings and
nobles (the line 'O king of Assyria' in v. 18 is probably an
explanatory gloss) is again familiar from Jeremiah, Ezekiel
and Zech. 9–14. Their citizens will be scattered like sheep on
the mountains, just like those whose leaders have betrayed
them (cf. Ezek. 34.1-6; Zech. 13.7). There will be none to help
and none to lament, for all have suffered too much at their
hands. This 'universalizing' of the downfall of Nineveh gives
force to Keller's assertion: 'The destruction of Nineveh is
taken up in myth' (1972, p. 417). Nineveh stands for every
tyrant of all times. That is why there is no one 'upon whom

has not come your continued oppression' (v. 19). Coggins concludes, 'Just as the unceasing evil of the oppressor has been universal in its effects...so the realization of God's power in the overthrow of that oppressor will be even more universal' (p. 59).

Further Reading

W.R. Arnold, 'The Composition of Nahum 1–2.3', *ZAW* 21 (1901), pp. 225-65.

K.J. Cathcart, 'Treaty-Curses and the Book of Nahum', *CBQ* 35 (1973), pp. 179-87.

D.L. Christensen, 'The Acrostic of Nahum Reconsidered', *ZAW* 87 (1975), pp. 17-30.

J. Day, *God's Conflict with the Dragon and the Sea*, Cambridge, 1985.

M. Delcor, 'Allusions à la déesse Ištar en Nahum 2.8?', *Biblica* 58 (1977), pp. 73-83.

G.R. Driver, 'Farewell to Queen Huzzab!', *JTS* n.s. 15 (1964), pp. 296-98.

J. Gray, 'The Hebrew Conception of the Kingship of God: Its Origin and Development', *VT* 6 (1956), pp. 268-85.

—'The Kingship of God in the Prophets and the Psalms', *VT* 11 (1961), pp. 1-29.

H. Gunkel, 'Nahum 1', *ZAW* 13 (1893), pp. 223-44.

A. Haldar, 'Studies in the Book of Nahum', *Uppsala Universitets Årskrift*, Uppsala, Leipzig, 1946.

J. Jeremias, *Kultprophetie und Gerichtsverkündigung in der späten Königszeit Israels*, WMANT 35, Heidelberg, 1970.

C. Keller, 'Die theologische Bewältigung der geschichtlichen Wirklichkeit in der Prophetie Nahums', *VT* 22 (1972), pp. 339-419.

H.W.F. Saggs, 'Nahum and the Fall of Nineveh', *JBL* 20 (1969), pp. 220-25.

H. Schulz, *Das Buch Nahum*, BZAW 129, 1973.

S.J. de Vries, 'The Acrostic of Nahum in the Jerusalem Liturgy', *VT* 16 (1966), pp. 476-81.

W.C. van Wyk, 'Allusions to "Prehistory" and History in the Book of Nahum', in *De Fructu Oris Sui: Essays in Honour of Adrianus van Selms*, ed. I.H. Eybers *et al.*, Pretoria Oriental Series 9, Leiden, 1971.

4

THE POETIC
STYLE

TO GIVE ONLY A SUMMARY of the thematic contents of the book of Nahum would be to do it an injustice. Whatever other limitations it may be charged with, it expresses its ideas in vigorous, imaginative, lively poetry which makes it something of a literary masterpiece. If, as has been said, 'metaphor is the lifeblood of poetry', then the blood flows vigorously here. The oppressor nation is a lion in its den (2.11f. [12f.]), or, again, a prostitute (3.4). The shock of Yahweh's judgment produces the staggering and helplessness of drunkenness (3.11). Similes abound. God's victims are swept away like stubble before God's wrath which burns like fire (1.12). The cries of the captive women sound like the moaning of doves (2.7 [8]). The city is like a pool of water evaporating in the sun (2.8 [9]). The people are like locusts for number (3.15) but they are driven from their refuge by the blazing heat of the sun (3.16). The literary device of the rhetorical question sharpens the irony: 'Who can stand before his indignation?' (1.6); 'Where is the lion's den?' (2.11 [12]); 'Are you better than No-Amôn?' (3.8). The speed and tumult of the advance is captured in a series of terse infinitives functioning as imperatives:

> Fortify the rampart,
> guard the way,
> gird your loins,
> summon up all your strength
> (2.2 [3]—in this Chapter I give my own translation).

The heat and fury of the battle live in a series of impressionistic 'shots' of the march:

> The crack of the whip
> and the vibrating of the wheels,
> the galloping horse
> and the jolting chariot;
> the horseman rising up,
> the blazing sword,
> the flashing spear ... (3.2f.).

Repetition drives home the threats with relentless hammer blows:

> Even (*gam*) she (Thebes) was destined for exile ...
> Even (*gam*) her children were dashed in pieces ...
> Even (*gam*) you shall become drunk ...
> Even (*gam*) you shall seek refuge from the enemy (3.10f.).

Something of the tone of the whole book is set by the three times repeated 'avenging' as a description of Yahweh in 1.2. The totality of judgment is emphasized by the striking number of times the word 'no' or 'none' (Heb. *'ên*) occurs. There is 'no turning back' (2.8 [9]), 'no end to the stores' (2.9 [10]), 'none to disturb' (2.11 [12]), 'no end to the bodies' (3.3), Cush and Egypt helped her with 'no' limit (3.9) and finally there will be 'no alleviation of your disaster' (3.19).

Other features of the poetry less easy to appreciate in translation include assonance, e.g. *sîrîm ... s^{e}bukîm*, perhaps meaning 'entangled thorns' and *k^{e}sob'ām ... s^{e}bû'îm*, 'saturated with their drinking' (1.10); alliteration, *b^{e}qāqûm ... bōq^{e}qîm*, 'their plunderers have stripped them' (2.2 [3]). Play on words also occurs most strikingly in 2.3[4], where, *m^{e}oddām*, meaning 'reddened' in the phrase 'the shield of their warriors is reddened', recalls the Hebrew word for 'Edom' (cf. Isa. 63.1 where the same play on words occurs). This again, therefore, has the effect of extending the reference to 'Nineveh' in a more general way to all Israel's traditional enemies. It is a characteristic of late exilic and early post-exilic literature to make the name of 'Edom' serve in this way.

Whatever the message of Nahum, it has lost nothing and gained a great deal in the forceful, lively and dramatic expression of the poetry which serves it.

5
THE HISTORY
OF CRITICISM

WITH THE RISE OF HISTORICAL CRITICISM most attention in the nineteenth century was focused on the unity of the book, the historical and geographical location of Nahum the prophet and, increasingly, on the religious value of the book. More recently interest has tended to centre more on the nature and function of the material in the book and its place within the phenomenon of Old Testament prophecy as a whole. Bertholdt in his *Introduction to the Old Testament* (1814) believed that all three chapters came from the same author but were independent of each other, having been written on different occasions. Gunkel (1893), as we have seen, believed that ch. 1, including 1.15 [2.1] and 2.2 [3], was independent and from a later author. It was not a 'prophetic vision' but a psalm in the manner of prophecy (*nachprophetischer*, p. 242) dealing with the day of Yahweh. It pictured the theophany not as occurring in historical times but as it was received in the poetic tradition. Arnold (1901) also saw the acrostic poem as the work of a later (inefficient) redactor, attributing 1.2-10, 12b, 13, 14a, 15ab [2.1ab] to him. Many commentators have followed these scholars on various grounds, either because the acrostic form has seemed to them too artificial for such a lively and original poet as Nahum or because there is no specific reference to Nineveh as there is in chs. 2–3. These include Nowack (1897), S.R. Driver (1906), and van Hoonacker (1908). Amongst more recent writers, Renaud (1987, pp. 263f.) sees the acrostic hymn as 'without doubt later than Nahum' and gives as ground the absence of all allusion to Nineveh, an almost priestly solemnity of style very different from the more lively and concrete style of the remainder, and the fact that the acrostic form is not attested any earlier than the exilic Lamentations. The theological perspective is cosmic and universalist (vv. 5-7). The contrast is no longer between Judah and Assyria but between the faithful and apostate among the author's own people. Taylor (1956) dates the hymn as late as the third or second centuries BCE and notes that its literary quality is 'decidedly inferior' to what follows, and Elliger (1964) is also inclined to date it later. However, Christensen (1975, p. 27) believed that it was not a late addition but 'an integral part of the original composition'. He based his results largely on a study of the metrical nature of Hebrew poetry. Whatever sympathy we may have with his conclusions, we must be careful when attempting to date the material on such a basis, especially as Christensen claims to be able to trace 'conscious archaisms' in the poetry. While this view is hallowed by what may be termed the 'F.M. Cross school' of biblical studies, it really loses all control over the method. How are we reliably to distinguish between genuinely ancient poetry and later composition which contains 'conscious archaisms'? A number of commentators agree on the integrity of the poem, however, including R.L. Smith (1984). Achtemeier (1986) thought that the author 'borrowed' the hymn (p. 6).

As long ago as 1902, K. Budde said that 2.4–3.7 has been subject to later revision and so raised the question of the unity and integrity of the rest of the material in the book. Wellhausen believed that 1.13, 15 [2.1] and 2.2 [3] are additions. Traditionally there has been greater agreement over the integrity of the poems of chs. 2 and 3. Eissfeldt (1964) for example, spoke for many when he wrote, 'In general the book appears quite clearly genuine'. He left open for question only the 'fragment' of the poem in 1.2-9. There have, however, been two major challenges to this general consensus. J. Jeremias argued that the book as it stands belongs to the late exilic or early post-exilic period. Parallels with Second Isaiah, in his view, reveal dependence on the exilic prophet (p. 14). Original oracles of Nahum are to be found in 1.11, 14; 2.1 [2f.], 3.1-5 and 3.8-11, and these were all directed against Judah and Jerusalem. During the exile, however, they were taken over by cult prophets and directed against Israel's enemies, in this case typified by Assyria. One might legitimately ask why Assyria and not Babylon, if the Babylonian exile were the setting for the book and were as heavily influenced by Second Isaiah as Jeremias claims. Perhaps, he argues, this is because there was some anti-Assyrian element in the Nahum tradition and because the fate of Assyria was known. That is why it could become a 'type' of how the pride of all human powers, even that of Babylon, was to fall before Yahweh's judgment.

The other scholar who has argued for a later date for the book as we have it is Schulz (1973). The sub-title of his book is 'A redaction-critical investigation', and he applies the methods of redaction criticism with great vigour and in much detail. The opening theophany hymn consists of 1.2a, 3b-6. Verses 2b, 3a and 7f. are later additions. Verses 9f. comprise an expansion to the hymn. 1.11–2.2 [3] includes oracles of salvation addressed to Judah (1.12aαβ, 13, 15 [2.1]). 3.1, 1.11 and 2.2 [3] together represent the dislocated final stanza of a poem against the city. The second stanza consists of 2.6aα, 5b, 4, 5a [7aα, 6b, 5, 6a] 3.2, 3. The third includes 2.6aβbα, 9bβ, 8aα, 6bβ, 4aβ, 8aαbα, 7, 9abα, 10; 2.11 acts as a connecting link to a 'ring composition' which continues from 2.12 [13] to 3.6 and which has a complex redactional structure of its own. The last section is the mocking lament of 3.7-19 which itself has an introduction, two stanzas and a conclusion. 3.15aγ-17 and 19 are expansions within this. The final work is post-exilic since its various parts echo Isa. 14, 15, 23, Jer. 48–50, and Ezek. 26f. It depicts a universal judgment and is an eschatological prophetic hymn like the eschatological hymns in Second Isaiah. It comes from a post-exilic group which maintained and passed on the prophetic traditions.

Claims to be able to trace so complex a redactional process down to such fine detail as that of Schulz must be regarded as a *reductio ad absurdum* of the method; and all Hillers's objections to the methods of redactional criticism in the study of the book of Micah apply here. No doubt it is for this reason that Schulz's conclusions have been largely either rejected or ignored. This is unfortunate, for the parallels he finds with later prophecy do exist, as has been shown in our own survey of the contents, and some explanation of them is needed.

As to the date of Nahum himself, scholars remain divided as to whether he predicted the fall of Nineveh before it happened or was reflecting on it after the event. Christensen believes that the prophecy is a good deal earlier than 612 BCE, perhaps as early as 650; and Keller also dates it early. Elliger, Horst and van Wyk all agree that it pre-dates the fall of Nineveh. At the other extreme is J. Haupt (*JBL* 26 [1907], pp. 1-53) who said that the book was a liturgical celebration of the victory over Nicanor on 13th Adar, 161 BCE by the Jews who were suffering under Syrian persecution. 'He that shatters in pieces' (2.1 [2]) was Judas Maccabaeus. Not many have felt able to follow such confident precision in dating; but others have argued that the book represents some kind of celebration of the fall of Nineveh. Bentzen (*Introduction*, 1952[2]) said that, whatever the original setting of Nahum's poems, the book as a whole was shaped into its present form for use as a liturgy celebrating Assyria's overthrow. De Vries (1966) agrees.

Clearly it is impossible to be certain from the contents whether Nahum's prophecy anticipated and foretold the fall of Nineveh or was written in the light of its destruction. Bentzen's work, nevertheless, signalled an approach to the book different from those which had concentrated primarily on questions of unity, integrity and date. More recently a number of scholars have tended to ask questions relating to the nature and function of the material. P. Humbert (*ZAW* 44 [1926], pp. 226-80; *RHPR* 12 [1932], pp. 1-15) paved the way here by saying that 1.1–2.2 [3] was not an anticipation of the ruin of Nineveh but a prophetic liturgy, a cultic celebration of its fall in the year it happened. Since the call to keep the festival in 1.15 [2.1] posits that it was an existing and known cultic occasion, it is most natural to assume that it was composed for use at the New Year Festival in 612 BCE (although Humbert admits this must remain hypothetical). This view was accepted by Sellin in his *Introduction* and appeared in the 1929 edition of his commentary on 'The Twelve'. In his 1926 article Humbert had applied it only to the psalm of 1.1–2.2 [3]; but in 1932 he suggested that 2.3-10 [4-11] gives such graphic (Humbert used the word 'cinématographique') details of the

fall of the city that this also had to be assigned to the cultic celebration, while 3.8-17 and 18f., likening its fall to the fall of
Thebes, also suggests retrospect. He therefore believed that the
whole work was a cultic hymn affirming the universal sovereignty of God. Yet the variety of material—question, answer,
oracle, lament—all suggest that it was the hymn of a cultic liturgy, and Humbert likened it to some Psalms where 'the
oracular element of divine address interacted with the pray-
ers, lament and praises of the worshipping community' (cf.
Pss. 81.6; 85.8 [9]; 95.7; and Hab. 3.16).

We have discussed above that rather difficult-to-define
genre of 'prophetic liturgy', and it has to be said that there is
nothing here akin to such passages as Hosea 14 or Joel 1–2.
For example, no prayer or lament material is provided for the
congregation. Yet Humbert's point that there appears to have
been a tradition of *temple prophecy* in which the divine word
was addressed to the people in a time of need has been widely
recognized. This is, as he said, found in the Psalms and in other
prophetic collections, not least in Second Isaiah in which so
much material seems to be answer to the people's laments,
their cries for divine justice and help (see Whybray, 1975,
pp. 29ff., 62ff.). Some have therefore been cautious in accepting Humbert's specific claim about the occasion for which it
was composed while expressing sympathy for his general
approach. Schulz (1973) says guardedly that the middle section (2.12 [13]–3.6) might have been associated with a cultic
celebration of the fall of Nineveh, but refuses to assign it to any
specific festival. Keller (1972) sees the book, with its abrupt
changes of persons addressed and transitions to new thoughts
and motifs, as representing a dialogue between the prophet
and his hearers. However, Jeremias (1970) observed that the
oracles against Assyria and Nineveh fit badly into any alleged
cultic setting. Curses are not found there, and the vocabulary
and imagery are drawn from secular war and not from the
language of the 'Yahweh war' or the 'holy war'. However, he
was comparing them more especially with the role played by
the oracles against the nations in Old Testament prophecy as
such rather than with the particular issues raised by Bentzen,
Humbert and Schulz. Eaton (1981, pp. 14-21) has enthusiasti-
cally endorsed the views of the latter. He asserts that Nahum

spoke during an autumn festival. This is demonstrated 'by his dominant images and themes—Yahweh's advent to fight chaos (Belial), and the messengers bringing tidings of victory with a summons to fulfil vows and celebrate the pilgrimage feast' (p. 15).

There has been no fuller or more systematic investigation of the mythological motifs in Nahum's language and imagery than that by Haldar (1946). Such imagery, he claims, formed the bones and sinews of the liturgical worship of the Jerusalem temple and hence finds expression in many psalms as well as in many of the prophetic collections. This is particularly so in the later, more eschatological 'apocalyptic' type expectations. Myth is the material by which alone *Urzeit* and *Endzeit* (the time before this world's recorded history began and the time following it) can be expressed. Yet Haldar, for all that he was the first to establish the case for cultic, temple prophets (1945), was cautious in his conclusions. He rejected Humbert's claim (and that of Haupt who had associated the book with a cultic celebration of a victory in 161 BCE) that it could be linked to a particular cultic occasion. The book is not of liturgical type or composition, but it is built so consistently on cultic motifs that it may well derive from cultic circles who were familiar with the ritual texts and were themselves transmitters of those texts (p. 148).

This has been the view of one of the most recent commentators on Nahum, Coggins (1982, 1985). He argues throughout for a strong cultic background to much of the language and symbolism found in the book. This, rather than direct quotations by one source from another, accounts for many of the parallels to be found with other prophetic writings. So 'it is right to recognize that the literary usage of Nahum may often imply an indebtedness to the language of the cult' (1985, p. 10). It is difficult, however, to go much farther than that and assert that Nahum was himself 'a cult prophet' or, certainly, to assign the book to one particular cultic event, owing to our lack of detailed knowledge of the Jerusalem temple worship and lack of agreement as to the precise role of the temple prophets in that worship (1982, pp. 91f.).

Nevertheless, the parallels with our prophetic material, especially the later additions to the prophetic books and the oracles against foreign nations, direct our attention to questions of the nature and function of the material. Here Coggins is at one with those views we have just been considering. These views recognize that the book as we have it is the result of later redaction and a complex process of growth (although we cannot hope with confidence to recover that process with the detailed accuracy which some, such as Schulz, have claimed). So Coggins can say, 'In so far as the redactional process underlying Nahum can be traced, it appears primarily to be concerned with drawing out one particular aspect of the prophetic message' (1982, p. 84). The place of the book in the larger 'prophetic message' has been increasingly the emphasis of recent study and appears to offer a more fruitful way forward than merely continuing to pursue old arguments about date and historical setting, since the text which we have is not itself interested enough in such issues to give ground for sure conclusions.

Further Reading

A. Bentzen, *Introduction to the Old Testament*, Copenhagen, 5th edn, 1959.

R.J. Coggins, 'An Alternative Prophetic Tradition?', *Israel's Prophetic Traditions*, ed. R.J. Coggins and others, Cambridge, 1982.

S.R. Driver, *The Minor Prophets: Nahum, Habakkuk, Zephaniah, Haggai, Zechariah, Malachi*, Century Bible, 1906.

J. Eaton, *Vision in Worship*, London, 1981.

O. Eissfeldt, *The Old Testament: An Introduction*, Oxford, 1965.

A.S. van Hoonacker, *Les douze petits prophètes*, Etudes Bibliques, Paris, 1908.

W. Nowack, *Die kleinen Propheten übersetzt and erklärt*, HAT, 1903[2].

R.N. Whybray, *Isaiah 40–66*, NCB, London, 1975.

6

THE FUNCTION
AND MESSAGE
OF THE BOOK

IT IS CLEAR, THEN, that there is no easy explanation of the way in which the book of Nahum attained its present form, what part, if any, was played by an 'original' prophet Nahum, and for what purpose the book was shaped and included in 'the Book of the Twelve'. It would be unduly sceptical to say there was no such prophet, or to deny that he lived during the time of Assyrian domination in the eighth and seventh centuries BCE or that he predicted the downfall of Nineveh. There is, however, nothing so specific to the overthrow of Nineveh in the breathtaking vivid description of that battle to justify Humbert's view (1932, p. 8) that the almost cinematograph-like quality of the description must be the work of an eyewitness. Any outstanding poet who had experienced any battle for any city at any time could have produced these poems. On the other hand, if the whole book was entirely an exilic work, one must ask why Nineveh was specified at all, rather than, as with Second Isaiah, Babylon, or even, in the way of much late exilic and post-exilic literature, Edom (cf. Mal. 1.2-5; Lam. 4.21f.; Joel 3.19; Obad. v. 8). Jeremias's attempts to meet this criticism lack conviction. It seems reasonable to assume, therefore, that Nahum prophesied before the fall of Nineveh and predicted its capture.

We do not know what the purpose of such oracles would have been. There has been a great deal of discussion about the place of the oracles against foreign nations in Hebrew prophecy. A brief discussion of some of the main views can be found in J. Barton, *Amos's Oracles against the Nations*, Cambridge, 1980, pp. 8-13, although naturally he deals there mainly with the special function of such oracles in the book of Amos. Whether they had their origin in the ideal of the 'Holy War' or the 'Yahweh War' (in which it was believed that Yahweh came to fight at the head of Israel's armies against their enemies), or in the cult, or whether they were a special form of 'salvation' oracle for Israel, it seems likely that they were seen as effectively bringing about the events they were proclaiming. Jeremias especially emphasizes this. Nahum, according to him, is not primarily an historian, but an 'interpreter of history'. Even more, he is a 'prophetic activator' in history (p. 415). By his announcement of Nineveh's overthrow in universal, mythical and symbolic language he is, by his prophetic word, releasing the power of God which will bring down all powers opposed to him. Jeremias is here speaking of the later form of the book, but with the implication that in this form there is a re-activating of the earlier words of the prophet which, as we have seen, he believed to have been directed against Judah.

That may have been the role of the historical Nahum. But, as we have seen, the evidence of the composite nature even of the poems in chs. 2–3, the theophany hymn in 1.2-8 and the abrupt transitions in 1.9–2.2 [3]—all these suggest that that role has been built on and developed. Remarkable parallels to Second Isaiah (1.15 [2.1]; cf. Isa. 52.7), the denunciation of the Assyrian worship of 'false gods', the assurance of comfort and deliverance to Israel and of the overthrow of its enemies, parallels to much of the exilic and post-exilic literature such as Isaiah 24–27, Trito-Isaiah (Isa. 56–66) and Zechariah 9–14 in the use of mythical language and imagery, the 'generalizing' tendency of the opening chapter as well as of much in chs. 2–3—all these, again, suggest that earlier material has been taken and given a new interpretation and a new thrust. As Keller (and others) have observed, Nineveh has become a symbol. The historical city of Nineveh may have given impetus to the book, but it has become 'a type of the pagan tyrannical metropolis' (p. 412) just like the 'city of chaos' in Isaiah 24–27 and Edom in much late Old Testament literature (see Cresson, 1972).

We have seen how such material could become part of what might be called the 'stock-in-trade' of Jerusalem prophetic circles. This is illustrated by the recurrence of a common oracle in Isa. 2.2-4 and Mic. 4.1-4. We shall also see, similarly, how common material is found in both Obadiah and the book of Jeremiah. Further, we have noticed how oracles of salvation for Israel have been added to all the major prophetic collections in order to relate them to the exilic and post-exilic situations. Further, the groups of oracles against foreign nations in these major prophetic books have to be set in this same category. It is to just such oracles that Nahum has been linked by the use of the word *massā'*, 'burden' or 'oracle', in the superscription. It seems that we must see the book of Nahum in this larger Old Testament prophetic context and understand it as serving the same function as the additional oracles of salvation and oracles against the nations in the other prophetical books.

Finally, what is the book's 'message'? As many have noted, it bears testimony to the complete sovereignty of God. There is no allusion to Israel's past history (this lack also becomes increasingly a feature of 'apocalyptic' literature). There is, however, allusion in 1.3 to the great covenant promises of Exod. 34.6, and there are strong attacks on the worship of other gods in the manner of the covenant theology and the earlier prophets (1.14; 3.4, 5). Cathcart has drawn our attention to the large element that covenant-treaty language occupies in the book. This harmonizes perfectly with the strong belief in the power and determination of Yahweh to intervene in the history of this world and the conviction that no human or divine power can stand against him—both underlying beliefs of Old Testament covenant theology. The language of the cult in which this is expressed has taken into itself much of the language and symbolism of the ancient myths—language which was used to describe God's initial act of creation, but which is now used equally to describe the fulfilment of his ultimate purpose for his world. This is yet another feature of the 'apocalyptic' literature.

It is to be noted that the 'enemy' is not just a national one. Nineveh, as it is treated in the final form of the book, stands for all that is opposed to God and is characterized by false religion and inhuman oppression and cruelty. There is enough echo of the old prophetic warnings against Judah (e.g. 1.8, 14; 3.1, 4, 5f.) to remind the people of God that 'judgment' or 'salvation' on the day of Yahweh is not a matter of nationality but of obedience. Keller has described Nahum's view of Yahweh as a power which makes for order (*Ordnungsmacht*), or, as we might say, for justice, since it is clearly a moral order which is his concern. Any declaration of faith that the ultimate purpose of God for his world is a moral one cannot be wholly superficial or misguided.

Yet, perhaps, some saw that this purpose might be achieved not only by the might of the avenging divine warrior but by mercy shown even to his enemies. In the Greek Bible (LXX) Nahum follows Jonah. Glasson (1969) has drawn attention to a number of striking parallels between the two books. They each (alone in the Old Testament) end with a question; both are about the same length; both refer to the great covenant declaration of Exod. 34.6; both deal with the fate of Nineveh, but each in a very different spirit. Glasson asks, 'Is the ending of Jonah as a question about Nineveh consciously designed to refute the implication of Nahum's final question?' (p. 55). We cannot know; but it is good to recognize that some apparently saw a sufficient connection between them to place them next to one another in the canon. Taken together, the two books say that in both judgment and mercy God is working out his purposes of justice and order in his world. Whatever appearances to the contrary there may be at times, in this world the last word will be, not with the apparently invincible powers of evil, but with God.

Further Reading

B.C. Cresson, 'The Condemnation of Edom in Post-Exilic Judaism', in *The Use of the Old Testament in the New and Other Essays: Studies in Honor of William Franklin Stinespring*, ed. J.M. Efird, Durham, NC, 1972.

T.F. Glasson, 'The Final Question in Nahum and Jonah', *ExpT* 81 (1969), pp. 54f.

J. Jeremias, *Kultprophetie und Gerichtsverkündigung in der späten Königszeit Israels*, Neukirchen, 1970, pp. 11-55.

C.A. Keller, 'Die theologische Bewältigung der geschichtlichen Wirklichkeit in der Prophetie Nahums', VT 22 (1972), pp. 399-419.

OBADIAH

Select List of Commentaries

L.C. Allen, *The Books of Joel, Obadiah, Jonah and Micah,* NICOT, Grand Rapids and London, 1976.

D.W. Baker, *Obadiah, Jonah and Micah,* TOTC, London, 1988.

L.H. Brockington, 'Obadiah', *Peake's Commentary on the Bible* (revised edn), London, 1962, p. 626.

R.J. Coggins, *Israel among the Nations: A Commentary on the Books of Nahum and Obadiah,* ITC, Grand Rapids and Edinburgh, 1985.

J. Eaton, *Obadiah, Nahum, Habakkuk, Zephaniah,* TBC, London, 1961.

D. Stuart, *Hosea–Jonah,* Word Biblical Commentary, 31, Waco, 1987.

J.A. Thompson, 'The Book of Obadiah', *IB* 6, 1956, pp. 857-67.

J.D.W. Watts, *The Books of Joel, Obadiah, Jonah, Nahum, Habakkuk and Zephaniah,* CBC, Cambridge, 1975.

J.A. Bewer, *Obadiah and Joel,* ICC, 1911.

W. Rudolph, *Joel, Amos, Obadia, Joel,* KAT, 1971.

Of the commentaries peculiar to Obadiah, Brockington's is too brief to be of great help; Stuart's evinces many of the virtues of the series to which it belongs but is selective in its treatment of the relevant scholarly literature, while Thompson's is of just the length and treatment to provide an excellent introduction. Bewer offers all the advantages of the ICC series but now needs supplementing with more recent work. Other commentaries have been commented on at the beginning of the section in Nahum.

1

OUTLINE
OF THE BOOK

IT MAY SEEM something of a relief to embark on the study of what is by some way the shortest book in the Old Testament. Obadiah consists of only 21 verses; and one might be forgiven for assuming that not too many problems could lurk hidden in so small a space. So it is a little daunting to find that many commentaries, books and articles vie with each other in quoting earlier comments about its difficulty. Jerome is often cited: 'quanto brevis est, tanto difficilis'. This might be loosely paraphrased as 'its difficulty is in inverse proportion to its length'. Rudolph comments: 'In spite of its small size this little book poses us with very difficult questions concerning its unity and time of origin' (1971, p. 295).

Questions for interpretation there certainly are, but the general thrust of the book and its outline are clear.

1ab   Superscription, assigning authorship to Obadiah and relating what follows to Edom.

1c-5   An oracle, either threatening a future assault on a proud and apparently impregnable power, or describing an attack which lies in the past.

6-9   A continuation of the threat (or description) applying it directly to Edom.

10-14   The ground for the judgment against Edom (perhaps 15b should be included in this section).

15-18   Oracle(s) concerning the Day of Yahweh, now seen as a day of divine vengeance against the nations (15a), including Edom. A remnant of God's people will be preserved on Mt Zion (17a) and repossess what is rightfully theirs (17c). They will be used by God as the instrument of his judgment against Edom (18).

19-21   A somewhat obscure prosaic addition identifying the territo-
           ries whose repossession has been promised in v. 17. It cul-
           minates in an assurance of God's universal royal rule from
           Mt Zion over 'Mt Esau'.

2

QUESTIONS FOR
INTERPRETATION

SOME OF THE MAIN QUESTIONS which the book of Obadiah poses for the interpreter may be listed as follows:

(i)   the relation of the oracle of vv. 1c-5 to 6-14;

(ii)   whether vv. 1-14 predict a judgment yet to befall Edom or describe an event which has already happened;

(iii) the historical occasion of the treachery of Edom re–ferred to in the book;

(iv)   the relation of vv. 1-14 to the more general and even more 'apocalyptic' passage of vv. 15-21;

(v)   how vv. 15-18 and 19-21 are related to one other, and thus whether vv. 15-21 are a unity;

(vi)   the relation of vv. 1c-5 to Jer. 49.7-16. It has long been realized that close parallels exist between these two passages, and this becomes clear when a comparative table of the two passages is set out (the translation is the writer's):

Obadiah	*Jeremiah 49*
1b We have heard a report from Yahweh and a messenger has been sent around the nations.	14a I have heard a report from Yahweh and a messenger has been sent around the nations.
1c Arise! Let us stand against her for battle.	14b Assemble and come against her and stand up for battle.
2. See, I have made you insignificant among the nations; you are deeply despised.	15 For see, I have made you insignificant among the nations, despised by mankind.

3a The pride of your heart has deceived you.

16a The terror you inspire has deceived you, the pride of your heart.

3b Dwelling in the rocky fastnesses, high his dwelling place.

16b Dwelling in the rocky fastnesses, holding the height of the hill.

3c He says in his heart, 'Who can bring me down to earth?'

4a If you soar aloft like the eagle and between the stars your nest is set,

16c But make your nest as high as the eagle,

4b from there I will bring you down.
Oracle of Yahweh

from there I will bring you down.

5a If robbers come against you, if night-time plunderers

9b If night robbers come,

5b how will you be destroyed! Will they not steal all they need?

they will destroy all they need.

5c If grape-gatherers come against you, will they leave anything but gleanings?

9a If grape-gatherers come against you they will not leave gleanings.

All these direct parallels occur in vv. 1c-5; but there are also more general connections: between v. 8b, with its threat to Edom's 'wisdom', and Jer. 49.7 where Yahweh ironically asks if wisdom has departed from Edom; between v. 9, which threatens the warriors of Edom with extinction, and Jer. 49.22 which speaks of their fear; and between v. 16 and Jer. 49.12, both passages describing judgment—of Edom and of the nations respectively—in terms of 'drinking'. Jer. 49.7-22 as a whole, like Obadiah, is a collection of oracles against Edom and occurs in the section of the book (chs. 46–51) which is devoted to oracles against the nations. There has long been difference of opinion whether Obadiah is dependent on the Jeremiah passage or *vice versa*. More probable than either opinion is the view that —as we have suggested in our discussion of passages in Micah and Nahum where similar questions arise—both were drawing on a common stock of oracular material.

(vii) The relation between Obadiah and the book of Joel and other Old Testament material. There is one marked parallel between the two:

Obadiah 17	*Joel 2.32 [3.5]*
And on Mt Zion there shall be a remnant, and it shall be holy.	For on Mt Zion and in Jerusalem there shall be a remnant, as Yahweh has said.

Other suspected parallels are more general: Obad. 11 and Joel 3.3 [4.3]; v. 15 and Joel 1.15; v. 16 and Joel 3.17 [4.17]; v. 18 and Joel 2.5. There is in fact a significant resemblance between the structure and development of thought in these two books, as has often been observed. This will be discussed below.

Further, a fairly general correspondence between Obadiah and Ezekiel 35 can be observed. In Ezekiel, the oracle against Edom picks out for special mention the action of the Edomites in betraying Israel at the time of its final calamity (v. 5; cf. Obad. 10-14). Just such a sense of bitterness towards Edom for its action (or inaction) when Jerusalem finally fell to the invading Babylonians under Nebuchadnezzar is also reflected in Ps. 137.7, Lam. 4.21, and, a little later, Mal. 1.2-5.

Interesting and instructive as such parallels are, it is extremely hazardous to attempt to use them to date Obadiah. Even if we knew which source was quoting the other—and it may be that each is drawing independently on a common stock of oracular material—we do not know either the date of the oracles in Jeremiah 46–51 or, with any precision, that of the book of Joel.

(viii) Such relationships with other prophetic material raise questions, not only about date, but about the book's nature, the purpose for which it was produced, the function it served in the community and its theological teaching.

These, then, are some of the questions which have to be faced when we try to unravel this little book. Rather than trace the history of criticism in some kind of chronological order as we have done in our survey of the book of Micah and, to some extent, of Nahum, we shall here sketch the main lines along which scholarly study has sought the answers to such questions. Since, however, the book deals so much with Edom, it would be helpful to begin with a brief survey of the history of the relations between the two peoples.

3

ISRAEL
AND EDOM

THERE EXISTED A TRADITION that Israel and Edom were somehow related. (The Edomites occupied an area to the south-east of Judah across the Dead Sea with the Wādi el-Hesā as their northern border and Wādi Hismah in the south [J.R. Bartlett, 1973, p. 229].) This sense of relatedness was projected back into the stories of Jacob and Esau as brothers (Gen. 25.19-24; 27.1-45; cf. Obad. 10, 12). We do not know the reason for this. It may have dated from the time of David's conquest of Edom when it was annexed to Israel (2 Sam. 8.12). Yet other nations subdued by David did not to come to be so regarded, and the accounts of David's brutal treatment of the Edomites would hardly seem to be a solid basis for a relationship (2 Sam. 8.13ff.). On the other hand, there were strong traditions that Yahweh originated from this region (e.g. Judg. 5.4; Deut. 33.2), which may suggest that there were ancient ties of which we now know nothing. Certainly, Deuteronomy at least calls for tolerance of the Edomites because of supposed past associations (Deut. 23.7 [8]; see Bartlett, 1977; Cresson, 1972).

In the reign of Jehoram, king of Judah (mid-ninth century BCE) Edom successfully rebelled against Judaean overlordship (2 Kgs 8.20-22). However, in the next century Amaziah of Judah again attacked Edom, defeated its army and captured Sela' (a prominent highland town), giving it a new name (2 Kgs 14.7). The Chronicler records another war atrocity to equal David's in Judah's treatment of Edom in this campaign (2 Chron. 25.11f.). It is the Chronicler also who mentions an Edomite attack against Judah in a time of severe crisis when king Ahaz was threatened from the north by a combined invasion of Syrians and Israelites with the intention of forcing him to join them in an anti-Assyrian coalition (2 Chron. 28.16-19, which also mentions an assault from the west at this time by the Philistines). Whether or not the Chronicler is historically reliable here, the notice reminds us that relations between the two neighbouring kingdoms must have been in constant flux, each looking to take advantage of a time of weakness in the other to assert, or re-assert, control over the border area.

The gravest crisis for Judah came early in the sixth century when the Babylonians invaded. After a three-year siege Jerusalem was captured and destroyed. Strangely enough, the Edomites are one people *not* mentioned as helping Nebuchadnezzar (2 Kgs 24.1f.), yet it was Edom's 'treachery' which left an indelible impression in the exilic and post-exilic literature. It is clear from archaeological discoveries that the Edomites moved into the Negeb (the desert area to the south of Judah), although it is difficult to be precise as to the exact time that this process began. The Edomites may already have begun to feel pressure from invading Arabs (who in later sources are referred to as Nabataeans). This pressure certainly intensified in the ensuing centuries, and it led to Edomite settlement in the southern desert area which thus came to be called Idumaea, a name familiar from New Testament times. The historian Diodorus Siculus (*Bibliotheca Historica* 19.94) says that by 312 BCE the Nabataeans had completed their occupation of the ancient kingdom of Edom. The early stages of this process cannot be precisely dated; but the process may help to explain Edomite pressure on Judaean territory in the sixth century.

The book of Obadiah could thus be related to any one of a number of possible historical occasions when hostility between the two nations broke out, either to one of those mentioned in the Old Testament or to one of which we know nothing. Some older conservative scholars like Keil, Orelli, Sellin, and Young associated the book with the rebellion of Edom in the reign of Jehoram, i.e. about 850 BCE. Some have thought it would better fit the 'treachery' of Edom at the time of the Syro-Israelite invasion of Judah in Ahaz's reign in 735 BCE, although others have pointed out that no capture of Jerusalem is indicated in the accounts we have of that campaign (2 Kgs 16; cf. Isa. 7.1-18). For this reason at least Obad. 11-14 would not have been appropriate then. Wellhausen supposed that Obadiah's interpretation of Edom's fall was related to Mal. 1.2-5; and, since Malachi was to be dated in the fifth century BCE, that it thus referred to some stage of the Nabataean invasion of Edom (1898, pp. 213f.). Bewer (1911, pp. 8f.) thought that Obadiah should be dated after the time of Malachi, since Malachi held out some hope of restoration for the Edomites while Obadiah spoke of their being driven to the very borders of their land by a confederation of former allies (v. 7).

However, the great majority of scholars have placed Obadiah soon after the fall of Jerusalem in 586 BCE. Its close parallels with the other literature reflecting hatred of Edom for its role at that time of disaster certainly seems to make that the most likely occasion for vv. 6-14. The description of Edom's action in vv. 12-14 is couched in a rather unusual Hebrew construction. It consists of a series of prohibitions: 'Do not gloat over the day of your brother, over the day of his alienation; do not rejoice over the people of Judah on the day of their destruction...' While this might imply an imaginative warning against such action in a judgment yet to befall Judah, its detail suggests hindsight, and it is better to take it with RSV as a graphic denunciation of attitudes already shown in a time now past.

Some scholars, however, have mistrusted any attempt to place Obadiah in a particular historical context. Bič (1953) argued that the book is 'wholly unhistorical' (p. 15) and that, in any case, the text does not yield sufficiently precise historical details to determine any historical occasion which it might fit. It is, rather, a cultic drama. Bič believed that it belonged to the 'Enthronement Festival' (which many scholars have believed was celebrated in pre-exilic Jerusalem) and to the liturgy of which the psalms celebrating Yahweh's kingship formed part (see Johnson, 1951, for a general account). This festival was believed by some both to have celebrated and effected the royal victory of Yahweh over his enemies (cf. Obad. 21). These enemies symbolized the primaeval chaos which Yahweh overcame in the act of creation (cf. Isa. 51.9f.) and are represented here by 'Edom'. As such, Edom typifies all nations opposed to God's rule (Obad. 15). Obadiah is not so much, then, a nationalistic book as one which celebrates the ultimate victory of Yahweh over all the powers of evil.

Few today share Bič's confidence in identifying the book as the liturgy of one particular cultic event. Wolff in his commentary (1977, 1986) nevertheless believed that Obadiah was a cult prophet, 'of a type active in the worship of the pre-exilic period...taking up sayings that had been passed down from earlier prophets, interpreting them and giving them a topical application' (1986, p. 11). His prophecy was linked with no specific cultic occasion, however, but was rather 'exposition' and 'development' for his audience of existing prophetic material. The message he drew from it was not hatred of Edom but 'the punitive justice of God' (1986, p. 22).

Several scholars have shared Bič's view that 'Edom' became a symbol for Yahweh's enemies in general (e.g. Coggins, 1982, 1985; Cresson, 1972). Whatever the precise original historical allusions in the various component elements of the book, these were clearly susceptible to continuing re-application in new circumstances until, as in vv. 15-21, the whole theme of the judgment against Edom is lifted up onto a 'universal' and 'eschatological' plane. We shall return to this in the final chapter, 'Function and Theology'.

Further Reading

J.R. Bartlett, 'The Moabites and Edomites', in *Peoples of Old Testament Times*, ed. D.J. Wiseman, Oxford, 1973, pp. 229-58.
J.R. Bartlett, 'The Brotherhood of Edom', *JSOT* 4 (1977), pp. 2-27.
J.A. Bewer, *Obadiah and Joel,* ICC, Edinburgh, 1911
M. Bič, 'Zur Problematik des Buches Obadiah', *SVT* 1 (1953), pp. 11-25.
R.J. Coggins, 'An Alternative Prophetic Tradition', in *Israel's Prophetic Tradition*, ed. R.J. Coggins and others, Cambridge, 1982, pp. 77-94.
B.C. Cresson, 'The Condemnation of Edom in Post-Exilic Judaism', in *The Use of the Old Testament in the New and Other Essays: Studies in Honor of William Franklin*

Stinespring, ed. J.M. Efird, Durham, NC, 1972, pp. 125-
48.

A.R. Johnson, 'The Psalms', in *The Old Testament and Modern
Study*, ed. H.H. Rowley, Oxford, 1951, pp. 162-209.

H.W. Wolff, 'Obadja—ein Kultprophet als Interpret', *Ev. Theol.*
37 (1977), pp. 273-84.

H.W. Wolff, *Obadja und Jona,* BK, Neukirchen, 1977; ET
Obadiah and Jonah: A Commentary, Minneapolis, 1986.

4

THE INTERPRETATION
OF THE BOOK

THE SUPERSCRIPTION of v. 1ab firmly links the contents of
the book with prophecy by the use of the word 'vision' and
the messenger formula, 'Thus says the Lord, Yahweh...' In
particular, it connects it with prophetic oracles against the
nations with the term 'concerning Edom' (see the comments
above on Nah. 1.1). No details at all are given about the man
Obadiah; the name, as we have indicated, may be a descriptive
title than a personal name. Often oracles against the nations
seem to be anonymous since many of them are clearly
additions to the prophetic books in which they appear, and the
close parallels with the oracles against Edom in the books of
Jeremiah and Ezekiel suggest that this material also is part of
a common 'stock', as we suggested above might well be the
case with the book of Nahum.

Verses 1c-5 form an oracle which begins with an invitation
to battle against an arrogant and self-confident power
(unnamed in these verses). The invitation must be seen as a
literary and prophetic device to make vivid the menace of the
threatening attack rather than a literal 'report' of which the
prophet has heard. The form has been discussed by Bach
(1962), who makes just this point when he says that it is a conventional prophetic form rather than a matter of an individual's poetic style. He believes that this conventional form
stemmed from the Holy War ideology, that is, the ancient
belief that Yahweh marches out at the head of Israel's armies
against his (and their) enemies. The fact that it is God's judgment which is being announced is made clear by the state-

ment that it is he who summons the nations to war (v. 1bc)
and by the placing of the proclamation of judgment in the first
person. The idea that God uses human armies to execute his
plans for judgment is another familiar prophetic motif ; it is
found for example, in Isaiah 10, where Assyria is spoken of as
'the rod of my anger, the staff of my fury' (v. 5).

It is to be noted that the power that is threatened typifies
'pride' (v. 3a). The idea of 'height', expressed here by the high
and apparently secure mountain fastness in which this power
defies attack, is a familiar symbol of human pride in the
prophetic literature (e.g. Isa. 2.12-19). The same note also finds
expression in the parallels to this passage in Jeremiah 49
(v. 16) and Ezekiel 35 (v. 10). The theme of Yahweh 'bringing
low' or 'driving to earth' (vv. 3f.) the rebellious and the pre-
tentious is yet another familiar prophetic motif. Verse 5 is not
entirely clear; but, by the likening of the attacking nations to
burglars and grape-harvesters who naturally leave as little as
possible behind them, the totality of the destruction is emphasized.

Two questions for interpretation arise at this point. Are these
verses describing what *has* happened or predicting a judgment yet to come? The question springs from the Hebrew
verbs which are all in the perfect tense. This tense usually
denotes an action completed by the time of speaking. Some
commentaries take this view and so see this as describing
some united assault on Edom either before, or, more often,
after the exile, perhaps reflecting the attacks on Edom by Arab
tribes. However, the majority of commentators understand
the verbs as 'prophetic perfects'. This is another convention of
prophetic literary style whereby the prophet is announcing an
action that he believes will take place in the future, but is so
certain of the truth of his revelation that he speaks of it as
though it had already happened.

The other question concerns the relation of vv. 1c-5 to 6-11
and even to vv. 6-14. In favour of the unity of the whole passage may be argued the continuity of form. All of vv. 1c-14 can
be described as first-person divine speech. Again, v. 6, although
with different vocabulary, takes up the idea of v. 5 of a complete spoliation of the proud power of vv. 1c-5. Again, while 1c-
5 does not mention Edom by name, the Hebrew word for 'rock'

in v. 3b is *sela'* which was also the name of a fortress city in Edom (2 Kgs 14.7). Against the original unity of vv. 1c-5 and 6-11 or 6-14 is the fact that the closest and most precise parallels to Jer. 49.6ff. occur in 1c-5 only (see the comparative table above), although more general echoes sound as far as v. 9. Edom is not mentioned in vv. 1c-5; and, while the description of the territory would fit the region of Edom, Bartlett counsels caution before we assume that *sela'* must indicate the particular Edomite city of 2 Kgs 14.7: 'it is not always clear that "the rock" in these verses is a proper name' (1973, p. 252 n. 55). He cites Nelson Glueck who said that there must have existed in the Early Iron Age in Eastern Palestine numerous sites built on more or less isolated prominences and known by the name *Sela'*. Indeed, the reference in v. 9 is not to *Sela'* but to 'Mt Esau'; and while v. 6 does to some extent take up the theme of v. 5, the following verses introduce new ideas all related more specifically to Edom, now identified by the use of the personal name of Jacob's brother, Esau (vv. 6, 8, 9 and, by implication, v. 10). Now former allies have turned treacherous. The strange Hebrew word rendered in RSV as 'trusted friends' (v. 7, where the Hebrew means literally, 'the men of your covenant—i.e. your confederates—*and your bread*') has been discussed by G.I. Davies (1977), who concludes that the text should read 'those who eat your bread', i.e. your allies, or kinsmen. Now, in this section, it is the 'wisdom' of Edom rather than its 'pride' which is threatened with frustration and destruction.

Verse 10 introduces a new, but related, theme, namely, the reasons for the divine judgment. Since the grounds of accusation are an integral part of many of the oracles of judgment, there is no pressing reason for assuming that this was originally a separate section, even though such grounds are more normally introduced as a prelude to the threat (Westermann, 1967, pp. 142ff., and especially 176ff.). The apparent inconsistency of vv. 10 and 11, in which Edom is accused both of violence and of inaction may be resolved by seeing v. 10 as implying that its inactivity was an encouragement to others to commit violence against Judah. It was as guilty and responsible as any active participant—'You too were like one of them' (v. 11d)—the Hebrew word *gam*, 'even (you)', gives particular emphasis to this point (see the comments on Nah. 3.10f. above).

To some extent the theme of the combination of inaction and vigorous involvement in Judah's final death-throes is continued in vv. 12-14, in which a vivid and striking literary device is used. This consists of a series of prohibitions: 'Do not gloat over the day of your brother...' Again this is a construction which raises the question of the temporal relationship of these verses to the calamity of Judah in 586 BCE. Logically it might seem that the crisis has not yet occurred and that Edom is being warned against such an attitude in the future. This is, however, most unlikely. The passage is so vivid in its detail that, while no doubt imaginative in its composition, it appears much more likely to be a literary device describing Judah's bitterness at what was seen as Edom's part at the time of its disaster. By making just such actions and attitudes a series of divine prohibitions, the passage underlines the enormity of Edom's conduct, not only in violation of the claims of 'brotherhood' (v. 10) but in flagrant breach of the kind of actions God commands.

We may note a poetic device also in the exact correspondence of the fates of Jerusalem and Edom. Jerusalem was violated and robbed (vv. 10f., 13), attacked even by 'allies' and 'confederates' (the Edomites) as well as by foreigners, and its refugees scattered to the borders (v. 14). This matches exactly the fate which is to befall Edom: robbery (v. 6), attack by allies (v. 7) and dispersal of its people to the border (v. 7). This adds weight to the near-scholarly consensus that v. 15b belongs to this poem and constitutes its climax:

> Your dealings (with others)
> will return on your own head.

It further suggests that vv. 6-14 have at least been shaped into a unity even if they were formed from originally disparate elements.

Scholars have varied in their views on the unity of this passage. Fohrer divides the section into separate units comprising vv. 1b-4, 5-7, 8-11, 12-14, 15b (1970, pp. 439f.). Coggins sees a new section beginning at v. 10, although he believes that, whatever the origin of individual sections, the book as a whole has been drawn into a unity by its cultic use (1985, p. 84; cf. p. 72). Wolff saw vv. 1b-4 as a 'basic text' of which vv. 5-8 was exposition and development, while vv. 11-14 contains a detailed indictment. Yet the whole of vv. 1b-14 was a single, unified discourse (1986, pp. 20ff.). Rudolph also conceives of all of vv. 1-14 as a unity, for 10-14 shows the moral grounds for the judgment threatened in 1-9 (1971, p. 296).

It is clear, however, that a major change occurs in v. 15. Rudolph summarizes the arguments for this when he says:

> In 1ff. the nations are the instruments of judgment, in 15a, 16, the object of judgment. In 1ff. only Edom is judged, here all the nations, although with particular stress on Edom; in 1ff. the nations execute judgment on Edom (1, 5) but in the second part, Israel (18). In 1ff. those addressed are the Edomites, in v. 16 the Jews (1931, p. 230).

Certainly we now see a switch of mood and emphasis. While there is a clear literary link between the two sections in the concept of 'the day', the word 'day' is used with two totally different connotations. In vv. 11-14 it is used repeatedly of the day of Judah's judgment and defeat; from v. 15 onwards it is the 'Day of Yahweh', a day of salvation for Judah's own people. These are now addressed by God (v. 16) and assured of a reversal of fortune and of role. Where they have 'drunk' judgment from God at the hands of oppressor nations, now it will be those nations which are forced to drain the cup of judgment (v. 16). The image of 'the cup' as either blessing or curse probably stems from the banquet-room where the host offers the cup to favoured guests. As such it would normally be a sign of blessing (cf. Ps. 23.5). However, it can also be a sign of judgment; and in this sense it is an image which recurs frequently, mainly in the later prophetic literature (e.g. Hab. 2.16; Isa. 51.17; Jer. 25.15). The reversal of roles will be complete. Unlike the mountain fastness of vv. 3f. and even of Jerusalem itself in bygone days (v. 16), Mt Zion will be a safe and purified refuge (v. 17). Unlike the complete pillaging which was to be Esau's fate (v. 6) and which had been Jerusalem's in the past (v. 13), now the house of Jacob will possess their true possession (v. 17). Where God has used the nations to bring judgment on Judah (v. 16) and, indeed, against Edom, he will now use the united tribes of Israel ('the house of Jacob', 'the house of Israel') as a means of judgment against 'the house of Esau'. Of Esau, unlike those who dwell on Mt Zion, there will be no survivors (v. 18; cf. 17).

The name 'Esau' provides another link with what has preceded vv. 15-21, occurring as it does in vv. 18, 19 and 21. However, the reference now to 'all nations' (vv. 15, 16), to the Philistines (v. 19) and to the Phoenicians (v. 20) suggests that 'Esau/Edom' has become here a symbol of all Israel's enemies, all the powers which have oppressed it in its history. As such, in their pride and arrogance they have ranged themselves against God as *his* enemies. It is nothing less than the final overthrow of all the powers of evil that is envisaged here. Of these, Edom was one powerful symbol (Cresson, 1972), and it is the establishment of God's universal kingdom on Mt Zion which is seen in vision (v. 21). One final twist to the fortunes of Mt Esau and Mt Zion occurs at the climax to the book. Yet this does not seem to be merely a nationalistic triumph of Israel over Edom, the final subjugation of troublesome Esau by his brother Jacob. It is the establishment of Yahweh's universal kingdom which is the goal, his final triumph over all the powers of evil. If the MT of v. 21 is right and it really is 'deliverers' who will go up to Mt Zion (some LXX manuscripts read 'those who have been delivered'), then the idea of v. 18 is renewed here. Israel will be the instrument through which God achieves victory. However, the kingdom will belong to Yahweh, not primarily to the Israelites.

The relationship of vv. 15-21 to 1-14 and of vv. 19-21 to 15-18 has been much discussed. Eichhorn (1824) appears to have been the first to question the unity of the book. He dated Obadiah to a time just after 586 BCE, but he saw 17-21 as a later addition from the time of Alexander Jannaeus (103–76 BCE). Wellhausen also saw vv. 15a, 16-21 as a later appendix: v. 15 'begins an addition which concerns itself with a general judgment by Yahweh against all the heathen which is carried out through the Judaeans' (1898, p. 213). This view has been often repeated, vv. 16-21 being placed by some in the Maccabaean period, if not quite as late as Eichhorn suggested. Some have seen vv. 16-21 as a unity (e.g. Myers, 1960, p. 150). Others have believed that vv. 19-21 was a separate, later addition.

That was the view of Rudolph who, even though he believed that vv. 15a, 16-18 marked a separate section, claimed it as coming from the same prophet as vv. 1-14, 15b, who had been an eye-witness of the terrible events of 586. That same eye-witness added the words of vv. 15a, 16-18, where he found comfort for his hearers in the words of his contemporary, Joel. Yet vv. 19-21 were the work of a later author of unknown date (1971).

Not all have followed this path. Coggins, for example, counsels caution on questions of unity and composite origin: 'it is doubtful whether so short a collection of oracles offers enough criteria for confident decision in this point' (1985, p. 89). Allen, (1976) in defending the book as substantially the work of one author, notes a parallel to which many commentators have drawn attention. The book of Joel also begins with two oracles apparently rooted in an historical event—a plague of locusts, which is interpreted along the lines of classical prophecy as a judgment by God against his own people for their sins (1.2–2.17). In this section 'the Day of Yahweh' is viewed, as Amos saw it, as a day of dark judgment for the people of God. However, at 2.18 the theme of the book switches to one of promise of salvation for the people of God. From that point 'the day of Yahweh' is seen as one of judgment against the nations, a judgment conceived in universal, cosmic, even 'apocalyptic-like' terms, while the deliverance of the people of God takes place on Mt Zion. In this section the 'locusts' of the first part of the book are apparently re-interpreted as a symbol of the enemies of God, an idea easier to establish since their advance is graphically described in 2.1-11 as the advance of a mighty army.

There are a great number of differences between the two books, notably in Joel's use of the 'prophetic liturgy of repentance'. Yet the general similarity of structure and development of theme is striking. The unity of the book of Joel has found powerful advocates recently, notably Rudolph (1971) and Wolff (1965). Allen (pp. 133-35) finds a basis here for arguing also for the unity of the book of Obadiah.

However, there is far from general agreement on the unity of the book of Joel, and while we should certainly take the parallels into account, this remains a somewhat flimsy platform on which to build arguments about Obadiah. Nor should we miss striking resemblances between Obad. 19-21 and Zech. 14 (Zech. 9–14 being a later, post-exilic work which can hardly be dated before 400 BCE). There also we find an earlier general prophetic motif of the elevation of Mt Zion (Isa. 2.2-4 = Mic. 4.1-4) trimmed out with detailed and somewhat laboured, even pedantic topographical details (Zech. 14.10). The same chapter, like Obad. 21, also contains a resounding affirmation of the universal kingship of Yahweh (v. 9). Such resemblances might suggest that both Obad. 19-21 and Zechariah 14 come from similar (later) circles who liked to expound earlier prophecy and relate it to the circumstances and hopes of their own time.

Further Reading

R. Bach, *Die Aufforderungen zur Flucht und zum Kampf im alttestamentlichen Prophetenspruch*, WMANT 9, Neukirchen, 1962.

B.C. Cresson, 'The Condemnation of Edom in Post-Exilic Judaism' (see Further Reading at the end of Chapter 3).

G.I. Davies, 'A New Solution to a Crux in Obadiah 7', *VT* 27 (1977), pp. 484-87.

G. Fohrer, *Introduction to the Old Testament*, New York, Nashville, 1968, London, 1970, pp. 439-40.

J.M. Myers, *Hosea to Jonah*, The Layman's Bible Commentary, vol. 14, Atlanta, 1960.

W. Rudolph, 'Obadja', *ZAW* 48 (1931), pp. 222-31.

W. Rudolph, *Joel, Amos, Obadja, Jona*, KAT, 1971.

J. Wellhausen, *Die Kleinen Propheten*, 3rd edn, 1898 = 4th edn, 1963, Berlin, pp. 211-14.

C. Westermann, *Basic Forms of Prophetic Speech*, 1967, London.

H.W. Wolff, *Joel*, BK, 1963.

5

FUNCTION
AND THEOLOGY

IN THE END, questions about the purpose the book was intended to serve and the message it was designed to teach seem more important and useful ones to follow than those which concentrate on historicity and individual authorship. We cannot hope with detailed precision to trace the growth of the book or the redactional processes through which it passed. We have only one form of it, and must make of that what we can (cf. the remarks of Hillers on the severe limitations of the methods of redaction criticism as they relate to the book of Micah), but we may perhaps trace a general development in the course of which the material was put to varying uses.

It seems possible that behind vv. 1c-5 lay a 'stock' oracle (compare its use also in Jer. 49.6ff.) denouncing the pride and arrogance of some threatening power and proclaiming Yahweh's intention to overthrow it by human agents. Such an oracle may not only have served the purpose of strengthening the people's faith that this would happen, but may also have been seen as one means of securing it. That is often thought to have been the use for the 'oracles against the nations' which appear in all the major prophetic collections and to which the book of Obadiah is linked by the words in the superscription 'concerning Edom'. This suggests that the home of such material may most probably have been in the cult and its use in the temple worship.

Such oracles would be capable of varied application in different historical circumstances. It is clear that at the time of Judah's death-throes, as it finally succumbed to the relentless power of Babylon and saw the unthinkable happen—Jerusalem, the very city of God, captured and destroyed—bitterness and hostility towards Edom boiled over. The two peoples, despite any ties by which they felt themselves to be bound together, had always had a tense and difficult relationship. What was now seen as Edom's indifference to their flight, and even more the calculated advantage they took of it, led to this oracle's being unambiguously applied to Edom. Both the superscription (v. 1b) and vv. 6-14, 15b reflect this situation: they make use of the older oracle to this effect. The same happens in Jeremiah 49 and, to some extent, in Ezekiel 45; and this probably explains the further, more general, echoes of the material common to each of these in vv. 6-9. This marks the second stage of the book.

As time went on, however, two things happened. Any immediate threat from Edom receded (although the memory of its 'treachery' did not). Further, the return of some exiles from Babylon, the rebuilding of the temple (completed in 515 BCE), and the renewal of the life of the post-exilic theocracy began to give rise to the hope that God had not finished with his people. Now, the passing of Edom's power became a 'type' which gave rise to the hope that God would eventually overthrow all the enemy powers who had ranged themselves through history against him and his people. The 'Day of Yahweh' now becomes again a matter of eschatological hope when God will, by means of his redeemed and purified people, defeat 'all nations', of whom Edom, and other powers, are potent symbols. He will restore Mt Zion as a place of security and as the seat of his universal reign, so that it will again be a place where 'his saints may dwell secure'. So ancient prophetic promises, like that expressed in Isa. 1.21-26, will be fulfilled in a great universal act of salvation. This is the hope of vv. 15a, 16-18, which must have been designed to fan the flames of faith in the post-exilic community.

Even later, as that hope continues to burn, 'preachers' in the temple round out the detail of just what that hope will mean, as they have also done in Zechariah 14. The people of God are assured of what 'possessions' will be theirs when God reigns as universal king (vv. 19-21). The same theme of God's kingship and the subjugation of the nations was the subject of much psalmody in the pre-exilic temple (e.g. Pss. 47; 93; 95; 96; 97; 99). It would be most natural to look to the restored temple after the exile as the place where such hopes would have been nourished and proclaimed again and given a strongly eschato-logical emphasis.

As to the 'theology' of the book, it is important to notice that, while it contains nationalistic hatred of Edom and sees 'all nations' as threat, the ground of Yahweh's judgment is not nationalistic. He is opposed to all human pride and arrogance, and it is this which he will bring down, wherever it is found (vv. 2-4). Furthermore, it is tacitly acknowledged that what God's people have themselves suffered was in fact a 'cup of judgment' from God's hand which could only have been for sins (v. 1b; cf. Isa. 40.2). What is envisaged is not, in the end, primarily national superiority for Israel, but the universal rule of God as king, removing from his domain all the evil which opposes him and thwarts his purpose. He will eradicate all that which 'Edom' and 'the nations' could be seen to repre-sent and of which they were symbols.

The faith that ultimately God will triumph over evil in the world and deliver the oppressed people of the earth is not an unworthy one. Further, we are not meant by those who admitted Obadiah to the canon of Scripture to take it by itself. Many have pointed out that it was probably placed where it is because it was seen as commentary on Amos 9.11-12:

> 'In that day I will raise up
> the booth of David that is fallen
> and repair its breaches,
> and raise up its ruins,
> and rebuild it as in the days of old;
> that they may possess the remnant of Edom
> and all the nations who are called by my name',
> says the LORD who does this.

The books of Amos and Obadiah, taken together, speak both of the truth of judgment for sin and yet at the same time of the hope and power of God's grace for those who have sinned. These continue to be the joint themes of all post-exilic prophecy from Second Isaiah onwards. By such faith and by such proclamation, the life and hopes of the community which was to produce both Judaism and Christianity were nurtured and maintained.

INDEXES

INDEX OF BIBLICAL REFERENCES

INDEX OF AUTHORS

Micah, Nahum, Obadiah

Orelli 93

Reicke, B. 35
Renaud, B. 10, 38, 42, 51, 56, 64, 67, 73
Robinson, H.W. 30
Robinson, T.H. 30, 42
Rowley, H.H. 22
Rudolph, W. 32, 42, 86, 87, 100, 103, 104

Saggs, H.W.F. 71
Schulz, H. 60, 61, 70, 75, 77
Sellin, E. 31, 76, 93
Smith, J.M.P. 30, 32, 41, 56, 57
Smith, R.L. 10, 56, 63, 69, 74
Stade, B. 28, 29, 30, 35
Stuart, D. 86

Taylor, C.L. 56, 57
Thomas, D.W. 10, 18, 22, 31
Thompson, J.A. 86

Vries, S.J. de 64, 70, 76
Vuilleumier, K. & Keller, C.A. 10, 56

Wade, G.W. 30
Waltke, B.K. 31, 41
Watts, J.D.W. 56, 86
Weiser, A. 10, 25, 32
Wellhausen, J. 28, 34, 94, 102, 104
Westermann, C. 99, 104
Whybray, R.N. 77, 79
Willi-Plein, I. 15, 16, 37, 42
Willis, J.T. 15, 16
Wolfe, R.E. 10, 18, 22, 30, 31
Wolff, H.W. 10, 24, 25, 26, 31, 38, 95, 96, 100, 103, 104
Woude, A.S. van der 25, 26, 33, 41, 42
Wyk, W.C. van 70, 76

Young, E.J. 93